Leopard Geckos
FOR
DUMMIES®

by Liz Palika

WILEY

Wiley Publishing, Inc.

Leopard Geckos For Dummies®

Published by
Wiley Publishing, Inc.
111 River St.
Hoboken, NJ 07030-5774
www.wiley.com

Copyright © 2004 by Wiley Publishing, Inc., Indianapolis, Indiana

Published by Wiley Publishing, Inc., Indianapolis, Indiana

Published simultaneously in Canada

About the Author

Liz Palika has written 45 books in the pets field; including *Turtles & Tortoises For Dummies*. She has written several books on reptiles, including iguanas, bearded dragons, turtles, and tortoises. Several of her books have won awards from Dog Writers Association of America, Cat Writers, Purina, ASPCA, and the San Diego Book Writers. She has about 1000 magazine credits, including *Newsweek, The Saturday Evening Post,* and all of the major pet publications, including *Reptiles* magazine. Liz and her husband, Paul, share their home with a breeding colony of leopard geckos, as well as a variety of other reptiles and amphibians, plus 3 dogs and 3 cats.

Table of Contents

"I think your Leopard Gecko is hungry."

Chapter 1

Leaping into Leopard Geckos

In This Chapter

▶ Looking at geckos worldwide

▶ Focusing on leopard geckos

▶ Examining their anatomy

*L*eopard Geckos For Dummies is for people interested in leopard geckos; essentially anyone who is fascinated by this unique, attractive species. You may be a parent buying your child his or her first reptile pet and want to supply a book to go with that pet. Maybe you're a kid buying this book with your own hard-earned cash. Perhaps you just bought a leopard gecko and need some information on getting set up as well as general care information. Or, maybe you already have a leopard gecko or two and just want a refresher on the best way to care for them. You may still be in the decision-making stage and aren't sure if leopard geckos are the right pets for you and your family. If any of the above applies to you, keep reading!

First Things First: Using This Book

Leopard Geckos For Dummies is a reference, so you don't have to read it in order from start to finish. Begin with Chapter 4 if you need basic set-up information, flip to Chapter 6 if you're trying to understand leopard gecko behavior, or head to Chapter 2 if you're still on the fence about adding a leopard gecko to your family. (Although those of you who prefer to start at the beginning and read until you reach the back cover are welcome to do so. I'll never tell.)

As you read, keep an eye out for text in *italics,* which indicates a new term and a nearby definition — no need to spend time hunting through a glossary. You'll also run into a few sidebars (the occasional gray box); although the information in the sidebars is good, it's not essential to the discussion at hand, so skip 'em if you want to.

While reading *Leopard Geckos For Dummies*, be on the lookout for these icons sprinkled here and there:

These are great time or money-saving ideas.

This is basic information for caring for your leopard gecko.

This is important stuff that can affect your leopard gecko's health or well-being.

Here is some advanced information that may interest you.

This small book is crammed full of information on leopard geckos, from how to decide whether this is the right pet for you, to choosing the right leopard gecko, caring for him, and even how to breed that pet in the future. This book can be your reference for many years to come. Just keep reading.

Taking a Look at Gecko Ecology

Geckos are lizards. They have four legs and are primarily (but not entirely) insectivores (they eat insects). However, those are about all the generalizations that can be made. Some geckos are ground dwellers while others live in trees. A few species of geckos live in arid deserts while others prefer more humid tropical environments. Most eat insects, but some also eat fruits and nectars. Many geckos are known for having sticky feet and the ability to walk straight up glass, but not all have this ability. Some geckos have immoveable eyelids while others do not. Geckos are amazing lizards, and it's this variety that makes them so fascinating.

Charting gecko evolution

Geckos belong to the family scientists call Gekkonidae. Ancestors of today's geckos thrived during the Jurassic period but unfortunately, fossils of such tiny creatures from that era are hard to find so their true evolution during that era is unknown. However, fossils have been found from the Eocene period (beginning 50 million years ago) that showed that the ancestors of today's geckos were adapting to many different habitats. In addition, those changes were occurring as those habitats themselves were changing. During the beginning of the Eocene period, Australia and South America were still one huge continent. It's amazing to realize that the ancestors of today's geckos survived such world-changing events as the splitting and relocation of two major continents.

The *family* of geckos, Gekkonidae, belongs to the *order* (group) of lizards called Squamata, and the *class* called Reptiles.

Mapping geckos around the world

Geckos today are found in North America, South America, Central America, Africa, the Mediterranean regions, Madagascar, Asia, the Far East and many islands in the Pacific. Some of these populations evolved in those locations, but many more were transported there as people themselves traveled more. Sailing ships and the intro-duction of world trade spread many geckos to the four corners of the world. Some of these reptilian travelers died during the voyage, of course, and many others died in the new locations. But the abil-ity of geckos to adapt to new conditions allowed enough to survive to establish new populations.

Today, geckos can be found in many different places:

- ✔ Tokay geckos are from Southeast Asia; north through Japan and up to Korea. Introduced populations have been seen in Florida.

- ✔ Tropical geckos (referring to their common name) originated in South Africa, and have been introduced and are thriving in Central America and other ports.

- ✔ Mediterranean geckos are from Northern Africa and the Mediterranean region, and have been introduced and are thriving in North America and Mexico.

Reptiles are identified by a scientific name (such as *Eublepharis macularius* and a common name, leopard gecko. The scientific name is used for accuracy, and the common name is used for ease of pronunciation (and remembering!).

Just as geckos can be found all over the world, they can be found in a variety of habitats and climatic conditions. The banded geckos of the southwestern United States live in extremely arid deserts, just as the leopard geckos do in Pakistan and Afghanistan. Yet the green tree geckos of New Zealand live in densely forested areas with high humidity.

Understanding different gecko species

All geckos have a similar body type. The legs are short, the body cylindrical but squat, and the skin has fine scales that feel smooth to the touch. Many geckos species may also have some *granular* (bumpy) scales that are small smooth bumps while others many have scales that are *tubercles* (more pointy) or *keeled* (partially folded). The head is usually large in comparison to the body although some species (such as day geckos) have a more stream-lined head.

Geckos are visual creatures, using their eyes to identify food and potential predators. Although many geckos will smell food before eating it, vision seems to be by far the most important sense. Those geckos who are *diurnal* (active during the day) have round pupils in the eyes, and those species that are *nocturnal* (active at night) have pupils with a vertical slit. The colors of the eyes, the irises, are often marbled in appearance, giving a very exotic look to the eyes. Some gecko species have moveable eyelids, but most have a transparent, fused eyelid that can protect the eye from minor injuries.

Geckos' feet have long been a source of amazement. The ability of many gecko species to walk straight up a glass window (or side of a glass cage) is almost unbelievable. That ability comes from adhesive pads on the toes of the feet. When magnified, the pads can be seen as bristles made of keratin (like our fingernails), and the end of each bristle is split. These split bristles allow the gecko to adhere to a variety of surfaces, including glass, and to move under overhanging surfaces, such as under the eaves of houses. Geckos that are ground dwellers, such as leopard geckos and Madagascar ground geckos, have fewer of these bristles than do *arboreal* (live in trees) geckos, such as tokay geckos and green tree geckos.

Many geckos have some other interesting characteristics. For example, one species of the New Caledonian geckos and several Australian geckos will, when threatened, spray a foul-smelling liquid from his tail. There appear to be tiny glands between the segments of the tail, and the secretions can be sprayed as far away as 30 centimeters. Quite a shock to the predators hoping to make a meal out of these small geckos!

Focusing on Leopard Geckos

Leopard geckos belong to one of the most primitive forms of gecko, belonging to the subfamily Eublepharidae. Except for one species, the geckos belonging to this family are *terrestrial* (living on the ground) rather than *arboreal* (above ground in trees or on houses). Leopard geckos and others in this family have moveable eyelids (although the lower lid moves upwards instead of the upper lid moving down). Another shared and notable characteristic is the fat, whorled, detachable tail that will be discussed a little later in this chapter. Scientists may have classified the leopard gecko as a primitive species of gecko, but that really isn't saying that something is wrong with them; instead, it is simply saying that while other species may have continued changing or evolving, leopard geckos are perfect just the way they are. As you can see in Figure 1-1, they are attractive, hardy, and well-adapted to surviving in their native habitat.

Thriving in a hostile land

The natural homeland of leopard geckos centers in Afghanistan, into Iraq, Iran and Pakistan, and into northwestern India. There are many mountain ranges in this area — some estimates state that 49 percent of Afghanistan is mountainous — but leopard geckos are found primarily in the arid and semiarid deserts and plateaus. In the western and southern regions of Afghanistan where deserts flow east into Pakistan and west into Iran, there is what the residents call the "wind of 120 days." In June through September, the wind blows almost constantly, bringing in intense heat, drought and sand storms. Whirlwinds are common, with velocities up to 175 mph (282 kilometers per hour).

In these harsh unforgiving conditions, leopard geckos thrive. To protect themselves from heat, sandstorms and drought, the leopard geckos hide and sleep during the day under rocks or other thick, heavy debris such as broken concrete, overhanging ledges or hard packed dirt or manmade objects. The sand and dirt under these rocks and debris are cooler than those exposed to direct sunlight, and so keep the geckos from overheating and dehydrating. In addition, if there is any moisture at all left in the ground, it will condense on the underside of the rocks where the geckos can lap it up.

After hiding and sleeping during the hot daylight hours, leopard geckos will come out of their hiding places at night to forage and hunt. Their prey are small insects and worms. Leopard geckos are also on the menu, though, and are often the prey of foxes.

Warfare has also taken its toll on leopard geckos. Throughout Afghanistan's history, from ancients times through the present, geckos have faced the horrors of war. Habitat destruction, either through the efforts of people fleeing warfare, or through the actions of warring people, has caused great harm to leopard geckos. However, as this book is written, leopard geckos are not an endangered species, primarily because of the efforts of captive breeding.

Figure 1-1: Leopard geckos are an attractive, calm, hardy pet species lizard.

Finding a place in captivity

Leopard geckos have been bred in captivity for decades, becoming one of the first truly domesticated species of lizard. Along with dogs, cats, parakeets and goldfish, leopard geckos have found a place in both our homes and our hearts.

History doesn't say when leopard geckos were first kept as pets; perhaps a young child in Afghanistan turned over a rock and found a pretty yellow, black-and-white lizard and brought him home. In more recent history, leopard geckos have been bred in captivity for many generations, producing calm lizards well adjusted to captivity. Since the early 1990s, leopard gecko breeders have been producing a variety of colors and color patterns, including yellow, orange, white, black spots, black stripes, jungle patterns and more.

Besides their attractive appearance, the appeal of leopard geckos also comes from their calm demeanor as adults (babies can be feisty) and ease of handling. Rarely do leopard geckos bite, and if they do, the bite rarely breaks the skin. When held gently in the hand, leopard geckos settle down quickly and will relax and even appear to enjoy brief gentle petting.

Leopard geckos accept handling well, but will try to bite if held too tightly. Hold the gecko gently, cupping your hand around the gecko's body.

Leopard geckos can also be easy to care for when their needs are understood, and their cages can be an attractive addition to their owner's home. Breeding can also be relatively easy, and baby leopard geckos are a thrill to watch. To be honest, other than being responsible for another creature's well-being, there just aren't many downsides at all to owning a leopard gecko!

Examining a Leopard Gecko

Physically, leopard geckos are amazing little lizards. Their entire bodies are geared to survival in a harsh environment, and obviously they have been very successful.

Seeing those wonderful eyes

As was mentioned earlier in this chapter, leopard geckos are very visual creatures. Their sense of sight is very important to their ability to hunt and obtain food. The movement of their prey (insects) gets the leopard gecko's attention first, the movement is tracked and the insect identified as either prey or not prey. The leopard gecko's eyes are well suited to this task. As nocturnal hunters, leopard geckos have vertically slit pupils (see Figure 1-2) that allow more light into the eye when there is less light available.

Another adaptation that helps them see in the dark is that many of the cones in the eye (which allow the eye to see color) have over time turned into rods. Although scientists are unsure as to whether

leopard geckos (and other nocturnal geckos) are able to see color —
or how much color they can see — it is obvious from their behavior
that nocturnal geckos do see movements, outlines and shapes even
in very low light situations.

Figure 1-2: Gecko eyes are amazing; much like cats' eyes.

Leopard geckos have moveable eyelids. Although most gecko
species today have immoveable eyelids (their eyes are always
open - like snakes) leopard geckos have retained the ability to
close their eyes. However, the eyelid that closes is the bottom one;
it moves upwards, whereas almost every other creature on the
planet that closes its eyes has an upper eyelid that closes.

Leopard geckos can also lick their eyes. You may at some point be
watching your gecko when all at once a pink tongue will appear
and give a quick swipe over the surface of an eye. Experts debate
why leopard geckos do this. Some say it's a cleaning mechanism;
the tongue is cleaning debris off the eye. Other experts scoff at
that, stating that the moveable eyelid does that. These experts say
the gecko is obtaining moisture from the eye. They can continue
their debates. What is interesting is the fact that leopard geckos
can actually lick their eyes.

Checking out those amazing feet

Arboreal geckos are known for their ability to run straight up a vertical surface or hang from the underside of the eaves of a house. These abilities (which make those geckos wonderful escape artists when kept as pets) are due to their feet. Numerous small bristles made from keratin line the feet, and these bristles enable the gecko to cling to just about any surface.

Leopard geckos do not have the vast numbers of clinging bristles that arboreal geckos have. As terrestrial geckos they don't need those bristles; instead, leopard gecko feet have evolved to allow the animal to cross sandy soil easily and dig under rocks. Leopard gecko feet have shorter bristles that lay sideways, and have shorter more cylindrical toes with tiny claws. So just as leopard gecko eyes have evolved differently than many other gecko species, so have their feet.

Many terrestrial animals, including leopard geckos, do not have an inborn fear of falling. Nor, with his feet, can your leopard gecko keep himself from falling. When handling a leopard gecko, you must keep in mind that he has no fear of falling so you can protect him from a harmful fall.

Discovering the unique tail

The leopard gecko's tail is narrow toward the hips, round and fat in the middle and tapering toward the end. It is also ringed, making it look like several rings stacked together.

A leopard gecko's tail serves many purposes. First and foremost, it is a counter balance to the head. A leopard gecko's head is quite large in proportion to the rest of the body, especially if you compare it to a mammal. Look at a dog's head in proportion to its body and then look at a leopard gecko. The leopard gecko's head is big; but this allows it to have larger jaws and so catch larger insects, and as a result, get more food and survive. The large tail acts as a counter balance, enhancing the gecko's movements.

The large tail also serves as a fat repository. When food is plentiful, the tail will become larger. When food is scarce, the leopard gecko's body will metabolize the fat stored in the tail to nourish the body. A healthy gecko will have a fat tail that is in proportion to his body.

The tail is also used in communication. This will be discussed in more detail in Chapter 6, but the tail is used to convey emotion, to signal a readiness for breeding, and for self-protection.

Leopard gecko tails are *autotomous*, which means the tail can be dropped or detached from the lizard's body. This will be discussed in more detail in Chapter 7. Dropping the tail is natural, and can serve as a life-saving tool for your gecko in the wild (distracting predators), but it can also be a severe shock to your gecko.

Because your leopard gecko's tail can detach, never grab your gecko by the tail or lift him by the tail.

Scanning the body

Leopard geckos are not large lizards, but appear stocky and strong. The body is cylindrical but slightly flattened, almost as if it was originally round, but gravity has flattened it somewhat. The skin is soft with small bumps on the sides and top of the animal. The skin on the underside is very soft without any of the bumps.

The legs come out of the sides of the gecko rather than underneath. The legs are short and made for short dashes or quick bursts of digging rather than outrunning predators. Adult leopard geckos can reach about 9 to 10 inches (23 to 25 centimeters) in length, including the full tail and when held, feel heavy for their size.

Leopard geckos in the wild have a base color of yellow with numerous black spots and splotches on the top and sides of the head, body and tail. Underneath is white. Captive breeding has created a number of other color patterns, including those without any black, white geckos without any black or yellow, or even brighter yellow or even orange markings. Colors will be described in more detail in Chapter 3.

Identifying boys and girls

Leopard geckos as adults are *dimorphic*, which means there are differences between the males and females of the species (see Figure 1-3). Adult males have a proportionately larger head and heavier body than do the females. Males also have a chevron-shaped row of large pores on the belly between the back legs just before the *cloacal* opening (anus). Adult males will also have two pronounced bulges on the tail side of the cloacal opening.

Figure 1-3: Males are heavier bodied than females; often with a fuller tail.

Chapter 2

Making Sure a Leopard Gecko Is Right for You

*A*dding a leopard gecko to your family is much more than simply bringing home an attractive yellow, white, and black gecko. You have to provide this lizard with a home that supplies all her needs for comfortable living, which requires some cash (as well the purchase of the leopard gecko), some of your time, and some space in your home. You need to protect your gecko if you share your home with other pets. And you need to teach the kids in the family how to care for and handle the gecko. To make sure you cover all the bases before you bring a gecko home, I explain exactly what you need — and need to do — in the following sections.

Committing Yourself to a Gecko

Before you bring your gecko home, consider how you plan to cage her and care for her; this means prepping your home, your family, and your pets, as well as your wallet. In this section, I discuss just how much prepping you need to do.

Duplicating nature

Geckos as a family, and leopard geckos in particular, are quite hardy and adaptable, and have been known to survive under some horrible conditions. But a leopard gecko thrives only when her natural habitat is reproduced in a captive situation (see Figure 2-1). If you provide less than adequate conditions, the gecko may live for a while, but will not be healthy, will not reproduce, and eventually will die.

To reproduce a leopard gecko's natural habitat, you need:

- ✔ A cage or enclosure (equivalent to a 10-gallon/40-liter aquarium or larger) and the space to set the cage
- ✔ Substrate (the stuff on the bottom of the cage)
- ✔ A heat source
- ✔ A thermometer
- ✔ Food and water saucers or dishes
- ✔ A cage cover
- ✔ Cage furnishings (things to climb on and hide under)
- ✔ A ready supply of the correct foods (insects)

Figure 2-1: A realistic cage that supplies your leopard gecko's needs helps keep your gecko healthy.

More can be provided, of course; I listed just the minimum supplies for healthy living. The larger the cage, the more room a gecko has to explore and hunt. The more hiding places and things to climb in the cage, the more exercise a gecko can get. However, if you supply less than the minimum I've listed, your gecko will not thrive.

Spending money

If you decide to add a leopard gecko to your family, you have to spend some money. So before you start picking out names for your gecko, take a look at the following minimal costs of supplies that get you started:

- ✔ **Gecko:** Depending on what type you choose, a gecko can cost you anywhere from $25 to $100. (See Chapter 3 for more on choosing a gecko.)

- ✔ **Cage:** An empty 10-gallon (40-liter) glass tank runs about $20.

- ✔ **Substrate:** Depending on the kind used, this can be as much as $5.

- ✔ **Heat source:** An undercage heater for a 10-gallon (40-liter) tank runs about $20.

- ✔ **Food and water dishes:** Plastic jar lids are free (plastic peanut butter jar lids work well), but more realistic plastic dishes will be about $5 each.

- ✔ **Cage cover:** If the tank is specifically for reptiles, a cover may have been included; if not, a separate cover will run about $10.

- ✔ **Cage furnishings:** Use stuff from around the house for free or buy specifically made furnishings at the pet store for $5 and up.

- ✔ **Food:** Food costs vary. As a general rule, when bought in small numbers crickets can be 10¢ each, although you can often buy them in larger quantities and save money.

I listed minimal costs above. You can spend much more. A glass tank can make an attractive leopard gecko cage, but you can find many commercial and custom cages available that provide very nice environments for reptiles who also make attractive furniture pieces. One advertiser in a reptile magazine displayed a coffee table with a glass top that also served as a leopard gecko cage. It was very nice, and I'm sure was quite a conversation starter when guests visited. Of course, it was much more expensive than a simple glass tank, too.

Once you set up your leopard gecko, ongoing costs are minimal. The cage needs to be cleaned regularly, so the substrate needs to be replaced. And since the gecko needs to eat, you need to buy food regularly. One adult leopard gecko can eat anywhere from five to eight crickets or other insects each day, with the amount depending upon the individual lizard.

Giving up some time

A leopard gecko can be a very easy pet for many people, especially busy people, because geckos don't require a lot of your time for initial set up or ongoing, everyday tasks. The initial shopping can actually take longer than setting up the tank!

Once you have all the supplies, plan on taking an hour to set up the cage, to get the leopard gecko in her new home, and to feed her. After you set up everything, plan on spending 15 minutes a day for straightening up the cage, feeding and changing the water. Once a week, plan on spending 30 minutes for cage cleaning, perhaps 60 minutes if you set up a miniature desert environment (see Chapter 4 for more on setting up your gecko's cage). Any time spent handling your gecko or watching her stalk and hunt crickets counts only as pure amusement and shouldn't be counted toward time needed to do work, such as cleaning!

Protecting your gecko from other pets

If you have a houseful of pets, you have to take a leopard gecko's safety into consideration before bringing one home.

Dogs, cats, and ferrets see geckos as play toys and can, without meaning to, easily kill small geckos. Other pets can also be a danger to small reptiles. Large birds can kill a lizard with a peck; rats can bite the gecko; and snakes can eat them. Once hurt, the chances of a leopard gecko recovering are not good. They are simply too small and in comparison with other pets, too fragile. To be safe, before you bring home your leopard gecko, make plans with your entire family as to how you plan to keep the gecko safe. These plans, more than anything else, can prevent an unfortunate accident.

You can also invest in cages that cats and dogs can't get into (see Figure 2-2). Rather than having screens on the top that can be pushed in by the weight of a cat sitting on it or a dog's persistent nose, these commercially available reptile cages have solid plastic sides, bottoms, and tops (one piece) with sliding glass doors in the front. But even glass tanks with screen tops can be safe if you place them where the dogs and cats cannot have access to the cage.

Never encourage or expect a leopard gecko to play with other pets. She is too small, too fragile, and sees other pets as predators, not playmates. Make sure that when you take your leopard gecko out of her cage that you put your cats and dogs away elsewhere. You don't want to be enjoying your gecko and have a dog or cat decide to play with her.

Figure 2-2: Your leopard gecko cannot defend herself from harm and must be protected from dogs, cats, and other pets.

Teaching children about leopard geckos

Although leopard geckos make great first pets for children because they're small, easy to hold, easy to care for, and non-threatening, don't think you're off the hook when it comes to teaching your kids proper ways to interact with their geckos. On the contrary, following some simple guidelines can make owning a leopard gecko rewarding for a child while keeping the gecko safe.

Depending on their maturity level, kids under the age of about 12 should be supervised when a leopard gecko first joins the family. Care of the gecko should be supervised for several weeks, and once you feel comfortable that the child's dedication and care follow the guidelines below, you can back off a little:

- ✔ Always wash and rinse your hands before picking up your gecko. Dirt, grease, soap, or other chemicals (even hand lotion) can be harmful to your gecko.

- ✔ Pick up your gecko correctly, cupping your hands around the gecko's body. Never pick up your gecko by the tail.

 ✔ Always wash your hands after handling your gecko. You don't
 want to risk your gecko making you sick.

 ✔ Don't let your friends handle your gecko. Let them pet her
 head gently while you hold her. Too much handling can harm
 your gecko, plus they may drop her or let other pets get her.

Everyone, adults and kids, should always wash after handling your
leopard gecko or after touching anything in the cage. Leopard
geckos are clean reptiles, but they are animals and do defecate in
their cage. Getting into the habit of washing just lowers the risk of
a potential problem.

Traveling Tips

Leopard geckos, even captive-bred ones, really weren't designed to
enjoy traveling. Reptiles get very stressed when their environments
change, and stress can affect their physical health, sometimes to the
point that the animal dies. Moving, such as when you move from
one home to another, can be done without harm if care is taken to
keep the gecko's traveling cage from getting too hot or too cold and
there aren't too many stops or detours along the way. However,
recreational traveling (vacation) should not include the gecko.

Never let a leopard gecko's cage (either everyday cage or a small
travel cage) sit in direct sunlight. The interior of the cage will rapidly heat up, killing the gecko.

If you travel often, either for business or pleasure, think about how
long a leopard gecko would need to be left alone while you're gone.
If the vast majority of your travel is for business and you're only
gone for one night at a time, the leopard gecko left home alone
would be fine. With food and water, your leopard gecko may not
even notice you were gone.

However, if you're routinely gone for more than one night, you
should either not get a leopard gecko, or make sure someone you
trust is willing to help care for her. A family member, friend who
lives nearby, or a neighbor may help you. More and more pet sitters will care for reptiles now, too. In addition, the pet sitter will
bring in your newspaper, get your mail, water your plants and care
for Fido and Kitty. No matter who you ask to help, make sure they
are reliable and know how to care for your gecko. It would be horrible to come home to a dehydrated and hungry leopard gecko or
worse yet, a dead one.

Check out the following two Web sites to find a pet sitter in your area: Pet Sitters International at www.petsit.com and National Association of Professional Pet Sitters at www.petsitters.org.

Enjoying Your Gecko for Years

Leopard geckos live long lives, especially considering their size. (Most small lizards live just a few years.) Male leopard geckos have lived to their upper 20s, with 27 or 28 setting longevity records. Females don't live quite as long, with some living to be 20 or 21.

With that longevity comes responsibility, however. Owners often give up their leopard geckos because the geckos were bought for a child and the child got bored with the lizard, or the owners became too busy or decided to get a bigger, different reptile pet. Other geckos are given up because the buyer had unrealistic expectations and thought the gecko would be a more interactive type of pet, like a dog or a cat.

Although you may not know what the next 20 years hold for you, if you have a leopard gecko, realize that he'll be around for about that long, if not longer. So, if you want a leopard gecko, be prepared to make the time commitment, not just on a daily basis, but also for her lifetime.

Making Merry with Multiple Geckos

Many new leopard gecko owners find their pets so fascinating, they make the decision to add another, and another, and another. Leopard geckos can be addictive. After all, I have, ummm, well, let's not go there! Before you add more leopard geckos to your family, check out the pros and cons of having more than one.

The positive considerations include:

- ✓ **Entertainment:** With more than one, you have more gecko antics to watch.
- ✓ **Colors:** You can buy several with different colors and patterns.
- ✓ **Sharing:** Each family member can have his or her own pet.
- ✓ **Breeding:** Obviously, should you decide to breed, or to allow breeding to happen, you need more than one gecko.

On the other hand, there are some negative things to keep in mind:

- ✔ **Social behaviors:** Not all leopard geckos get along, and fights can happen.
- ✔ **Space:** Since not all get along, you may need more space for more cages.
- ✔ **Cost:** You need more cages, more substrate, more food, and maybe even veterinary care.
- ✔ **Time:** Caring for more pets requires more of your time.

Before you make a decision, take a look at who gets along and who doesn't.

Battling boys

Boys just don't get along, plain and simple. Male leopard geckos begin squabbling when they're juveniles and begin fighting — seriously fighting — as adults. Males will inflict enough harm to seriously injure or even kill each other. Obviously, males cannot be caged together.

Males are often more impressive than females because they are larger, have a heavier head, and sometimes their bright coloring is more intense. However, if you decide to have more than one male, each will have to be caged separately from each other.

Girls get along

Female leopard geckos, on the other hand, are very social. Several females can live together quite peacefully. They will pile on top of each other to sleep, will chase crickets together at night, and even get along during breeding season. If you want more than one leopard gecko but only want to support one cage, two or three females would work well.

When housing multiple leopard geckos, start with a minimum 10-gallon (40-liter) -sized tank and add 2.5 gallons (10 liters) capacity per gecko. Three geckos should have a 15-gallon (60-liter) tank or equivalent-sized cage.

Deciding whether or not to breed

Although boys don't get along together, boys and girls do! Or more correctly, one boy and one or more girls do get along. Sometimes they get along really well, and a population explosion occurs. One of the reasons leopard geckos have been so popular in captivity is because they do breed so readily. Put a male and female together and, if their caging and nutrition needs are met and they were healthy to start with — boom! — eggs are laid. However, allowing your leopard geckos to breed should be a decision you make, not your geckos.

Purposefully breeding your leopard geckos, or allowing your geckos to breed, should be a decision you make with some forethought. Breeding takes quite a lot out of females and does shorten their life spans. In addition, there is always the possibility that a male and female play too roughly and one of the two may be hurt. And then after breeding has happened, you need to supply the female a place to lay her eggs, and you will need to incubate them. The babies, once they hatch, are quite fragile and need some very specific care and food (see Figure 2-3). In Chapter 6, I discuss reproduction in more detail.

Figure 2-3: Baby geckos are very cute but very fragile.

All these warnings aside, breeding your leopard geckos can also be a wonderful, exciting experience. When a baby leopard gecko pokes her nose out of a slit eggshell, you will be as proud as if you actual ly had something to do with it!

Chapter 3

Finding and Selecting a Leopard Gecko

. . . .

. . . .

*I*f you think that a leopard gecko fits into your family, lifestyle, and home (more on that in Chapter 2), you need to find a leopard gecko — and not just any leopard gecko — but the right one for you. Many places sell them, but because not all sellers are equal you need to find the best seller so you can get a bright-eyed, fat-tailed, colorful, and healthy gecko.

You may be wondering what makes a good seller as well as a good gecko. So to be sure you're not only getting a great gecko but also buying from a reputable retailer or breeder, in this chapter, I let you know what to look for in both a seller as well as a gecko.

Scoping Out Stores and Suppliers

When you buy a new car, you do research first: You do some reading, test drive a few models, and look around. Buying a leopard gecko, especially your first one, should be the same way. Granted the financial investment in a gecko is significantly smaller, but you will have an emotional investment in it very quickly. If you choose the wrong gecko (perhaps a sick or injured one) you will regret that choice almost right away. You have begun your reading and research here (Yeah!) but you need to continue that research before you actually purchase a lizard.

Finding a store or breeder

Many people sell leopard geckos. Since they have been *captive-bred* (bred, eggs laid, and incubated in captivity versus the wild) for many generations, there is no shortage of leopard geckos. However, yellow page ads or store signs rarely state that they sell leopard geckos, so you have to do some footwork to find the people or stores selling them.

Before checking the yellow pages, if you know anyone who has leopard geckos, quiz them about where they bought them and how the process was handled. If their geckos were healthy and well cared for, then go check out that store. If they had problems with the store, then obviously think twice about shopping there.

To find more potential retailers, use those yellow pages to call pet stores in your area. Not all pet stores carry reptiles so you can obviously cross those off your shopping list. When a store says it does carry reptiles, find out if it normally stocks leopard geckos; some stores do while others may not.

If a store does not carry reptiles or leopard geckos specifically, it may be able to direct you to a *supplier* (someone who collects from breeders and provides to stores) or breeder in your area who you can call. You can also find leopard gecko breeders through advertisements in reptile magazines (which can be found at your local book store or pet store) or via an Internet search (use the key words "leopard gecko breeder" plus your city and state).

Once you have someone from the store on the phone or a leopard gecko breeder, ask the following questions:

- **Where do you get your geckos?** If they come directly from the breeder, the geckos should be under less stress from traveling and changes in the environment. However, if they go from the breeder to a supplier and so forth, the geckos may be suffering from considerable stress.

- **How should geckos be cared for?** They should tell you some quick basics about how leopard geckos should be fed and housed. You can verify the accuracy of that information in this book. If no information is forthcoming, that means the person on the phone either is unwilling to spend time with you until a sale is made, or he doesn't know anything about leopard geckos. Be leery of that store because the geckos may not have been cared for properly during their stay there. Of course, if the information is incorrect, cross that store off your shopping list!

✔ **Does a veterinarian who specializes in reptiles see the animals in your care?** Many pet stores have a veterinarian on call who inspects new animals as they come in, or is at least available should an animal show signs of injury or illness. If no veterinarian is available, or if you are told that their animals never need veterinary care, plan on taking your business elsewhere.

✔ **What do you feed the leopard geckos?** If they feed the geckos live insects, such as crickets, mealworms and waxworms, great. If they feed the geckos canned dead insects (I talk more about that in Chapter 5) or dehydrated commercial foods, be skeptical about the health of their geckos.

✔ **Do you have any references?** If you are thinking of getting a gecko directly from a store or breeder, ask for references. They should be able to give you several phone numbers and shouldn't be offended by your request. Follow through and call the people, tell them why you're calling and ask if they were satisfied with the lizard they bought. Ask if they would go back to this person or store for their next lizard.

All pet and reptile stores are not the same. While some care about the animals in their care and do everything possible to keep them healthy, others see the livestock in their care as simply stock to be sold. If you can find a store where the people care about their animals, stick with them and give them all of your business.

Taking a look (and smell)

After you have a list of places to visit (see the section above on how to find stores or breeders), find the time to stop at each store and breeder (you may need to make an appointment with the breeders).

While doing your research *don't* allow yourself to buy a leopard gecko right now. Continue your research first to be sure you get the best gecko that best fits your desires.

After you arrive at a store or breeder, be observant and be sure to do the following:

✔ **Look at the cages.** The cages should be clean. Although geckos defecate in the cages, there shouldn't be several days' worth of waste inside the cage. The cages should also have furnishings: stuff to climb on and hide under. Also make sure that the cages aren't crowded. Although leopard geckos are social and several can be housed together, the cage shouldn't be overly crowded.

✔ **Take a deep breath.** How does the store smell? It will smell like animals but it should not smell dirty.

✔ **See if the animals appear to be healthy.** Look in quite a few cages (not just the leopard geckos), and see if the animals all look healthy and uninjured. There should be no wounds, no missing toes or eyes, and the animals should be bright-eyed and alert.

You should feel comfortable doing business with the store or breeder for years to come. So linger a while, listen to the store employees doing business and watch their animals.

Never buy an animal because you feel sorry for it or want to save it. That only encourages a bad business to continue its ways.

Ordering from the Internet

Internet business is big today, and it's growing. You can buy anything from a car to a leopard gecko and more. However, you need to be smart about buying a living creature via the Internet. You can end up with a half-starved, injured, sick (or worse, dead!) leopard gecko and no recourse to get your money back. A few sources for geckos via the Internet are listed in Chapter 8.

Use the following tips to make a smarter purchase:

✔ Take a look at the Web site and find out what its purchase process is and what your rights are should you be unsatisfied.

✔ Find out what you can do should the leopard gecko be in poor shape or is not the color or sex you requested.

✔ Ask for references, just as you did for the stores and breeders. Knowing someone who has ordered a leopard gecko from a particular Internet source and was satisfied can often make your decision-making process easier.

You can find many very reputable reptile sources via the Internet. Unfortunately, when you buy a leopard gecko this way, you are buying it sight unseen, and that's a big risk.

Finding other sources

Stores, breeders and the Internet are not the only sources for leopard geckos, although they are usually the most common. Here are a few other places to check out:

- ✔ **Reptile shows:** Reptile shows are really a lot of fun as long as you leave most of your credit cards at home. (It's much too easy to spend too much money!) These are usually held at a convention center or something similar and have many vendors and breeders displaying their wares. You can find these advertised in reptile magazines.

- ✔ **Rescue groups:** Rescue groups take in pets that are no longer wanted or can no longer be provided for and adopt them out to new homes. Your local humane society or animal control will know if there is a reptile rescue group in your area.

- ✔ **Herpetological societies:** Herpetological societies are clubs of people all interested in reptiles, and you can find clubs for all reptile owners — some that specialize in turtles, and some that specialize in geckos. (You can find one in your area by doing an Internet search.) Many times herp society members bring excess animals to meetings to sell or trade. Members can also refer you to reputable breeders.

Herp societies are great places to find out more about leopard geckos or other reptiles, depending upon the group's focus. Experienced members are always willing to share their knowledge or point you in the right direction to learn more.

Choosing the Right Gecko for You

Once you feel comfortable with a store or breeder, then comes the fun part: choosing the right leopard gecko for you. And it is fun. You will get to see and hold many different geckos of varied sizes and ages, with different color patterns and personalities. The hardest part of all this is understanding you can't take them all home!

Selecting a healthy leopard gecko

You can find leopard geckos with amazing colors, interesting patterns, and wonderful personalities, but if the lizard you choose isn't healthy, those characteristics won't mean a thing. First and foremost, your new pet needs to be healthy.

Giving your gecko a head-to-toe check

You should check the following areas to make sure you have a healthy gecko:

- ✔ **Body outline:** A healthy leopard gecko should have a smooth body outline. The body should appear slightly rounded (without being fat), and the hip bones shouldn't be showing. The sides of the geckos should be rounded, and the tummy and ribs shouldn't be sunken in. Don't choose a gecko with lumps or bumps under the skin. These can be abscesses, broken bones, or tumors.

- ✔ **Skin:** The skin shouldn't be dirty. If the skin is dirty or has caked-in feces, the cage is probably overcrowded, the gecko has a higher risk of disease or parasites, or he's just been poorly taken care of. Overcrowding can also lead to fighting between geckos, with skin injuries, missing tails, and missing toes as a result.

Look for any black, brown, or reddish dots on the skin. They may be lodged around the neck or in the armpits, and when disturbed, will move. These are mites. Do not bring home a gecko with mites.

- ✔ **Underside:** Some places have heat (or hot) rocks in the cages to provide heat. If used incorrectly these can cause burns on the belly. (See Chapter 4 for more about these heating devices.)

  You shouldn't find evidence of soft stools or diarrhea on the gecko's underside, or at the *cloaca* (also called the vent or anus). A healthy gecko shouldn't have feces caked around the vent area, nor should there be any swelling or redness.

- ✔ **Tail:** A healthy, well-fed adult leopard gecko should have a fat tail. Baby geckos haven't had a chance to gain enough weight to create a fat tail yet, so the tail will be long and thin. As the baby gains weight, the tail will thicken. By a year of age, the tail should be getting fat.

Wild-caught leopard geckos may not eat, or may not have been fed, during shipping and will have a very thin, shrunken tail.

A leopard gecko that has lost its original tail may have regrown a tail. That tail is rarely the same size or shape as the original; in fact, regrown tails often look deformed (see Chapter 7 for more on regrown tails). Geckos with regrown tails are usually considered less than preferred, or seconds, and are often cheaper. The regrown tail does not affect the gecko's health, although it does affect its looks.

- **Strength:** When you hold the gecko in your hand, he should feel very strong for as tiny as he is. If he struggles in your hands, he should feel vigorous. His tiny nails will grip your skin and should feel sharp and strong.

- **Eyes:** Leopard geckos are very visual creatures, they find their food by seeing the insects' movements, so vision is very important. A healthy gecko's eyes should be equal in size; they should appear prominent without appearing either shrunken or bulging. The eyelids should fit well around the eyes with no swelling. You shouldn't find any matter in or around the eyes.

- **Face:** The jaws should be symmetrical, and when the mouth is closed, neither the upper or lower jaw should jut out; a healthy gecko's jaws fit together well. The nostrils should be clean, with no matter, mucus, or bubbling evident.

- **Feet and toes:** The gecko's legs come out of the lizard's body on the side, rather than underneath. The legs appear small for the body, but appear strong, and the bones of the legs are straight. When the gecko stands up and walks, the feet and the toes should not turn under. Although the body does sway and roll when the gecko moves, the gecko shouldn't appear to be "swimming." That, unfortunately, as well as turning under the feet, are symptoms of metabolic bone disease.

The leopard gecko's feet and toes should be clean and free of any retained skin during shedding. If the skin is retained, it can cut off circulation to the toes, to the point that the gecko can lose one or more toes. (Leopard geckos have five toes on each foot.) A healthy gecko who sheds well should have no swelling of the feet or toes.

Assessing the attitude

Later in this chapter, I discuss personality and how to choose the leopard gecko with the right personality for you. But attitude is different from personality. Each individual leopard gecko has his own personality, but all healthy leopard geckos have attitude.

Luckily, a leopard gecko's attitude isn't obnoxious; they don't want to bite or scratch or escape all the time like so many other reptiles want to do. Instead, a healthy leopard gecko just has a bring-on-the-world attitude that's really quite funny in such a small creature. A healthy leopard gecko is alert and active.

A leopard gecko who doesn't feel good lacks that attitude and acts lethargic and sleepy (a healthy gecko, if disturbed while sleeping, will wake up quickly). Check to see whether the gecko moves when the other geckos are disturbed. If he doesn't react to his cagemates, not lifting his head, not getting to his feet, he's probably ill.

Avoiding a wild-caught gecko

Luckily, leopard geckos are breeding well in captivity so there is very little demand or need for wild-caught leopard geckos. However, some breeders still import a few to add new bloodlines to their breeding programs. The best of the imports go into these breeding programs, and the lesser animals end up for sale. The offspring of the wild-caught geckos (those imported for breeding purposes) are fine. They are captive-bred (bred after their parents were brought into a breeding program).

Unfortunately, many wild-caught lizards suffer through their capture and transportation to the point where you see them for sale. They may have been in very small containers or crowded together in larger ones. Often they are not fed or watered during transport. So when they are offered for sale, they are usually very thin, dull colored, and look unhealthy. Wild-caught leopard geckos also have a difficult time adjusting to captivity and are rarely tame enough to handle.

Always ask where the geckos for sale originated, and if the answer doesn't satisfy you, ask pointedly, "Are these wild-caught or captive-bred?"

Savoring colors and patterns

Captive breeding has increased the colors and patterns available for leopard gecko enthusiasts to choose from. The colors range from intense yellow, to yellow with hints of orange, and even white, all with different patterns of spots.

Although you may find several different colors and patterns in your search, Figure 3-1 shows the normal coloring of a leopard gecko: a yellow base coloring with black spots and splotches on the body (the yellow may be brighter on the legs); a white underside — a pale cream white; and a tail with black spots on a base color of white.

Just because the color of a gecko is "normal" doesn't mean that other colors or patterns are abnormal. Normal just happens to be a common color you're likely to find.

Figure 3-1: The normal leopard gecko coloring is yellow and white with black spots.

Choosing by size and age

The age of your leopard gecko can make a difference to the pet-owning experience. Baby geckos are wild and feisty and require special handling, which means first-time leopard gecko owners should bypass these babies. On the other hand, older lizards are just that — older, which means they won't be with you as long. So, your best bet is something in between.

Your best bet, as a first-time leopard gecko owner, is an older juvenile or young adult (6 months to 1½ years in age). These geckos have passed the difficult baby stage, but are still young enough to live out their lives with you. These geckos, though, may still have some of the baby wildness in them and need to be handled daily. With this handling (discussed in more detail in Chapter 6) you earn your gecko's trust, which makes him calm down.

Picking a personality

When you look at leopard geckos, choose a personality that will mesh with your own. Don't choose a feisty gecko if you're a little worried or afraid. Don't choose a gecko who's really mellow if you tend to be hyper. Find the leopard gecko that just strikes a chord with you.

Baby geckos cannot show you what their adult personalities will be like; all baby geckos are feisty. The males are especially feisty, opening their mouths, hissing at you, and maybe even trying to bite you. It's hilarious to see such tiny little creatures act so bravely.

By the time leopard geckos are 9 months to 1 year old, you can begin to see what their personalities will be, which is another good reason to choose one at this age (see earlier for more information on age). In general, most females are somewhat calmer than males. However, I've had males who were very calm and when picked up would relax in my hands. My oldest male, Grandpa, will rest in my hands, or on my shoulder, for as long as I would like him with me. At the same time, I've had females who didn't want to be handled at all.

Chapter 4

Getting Ready for Your Gecko

● ●

In This Chapter

▶ Preparing for your gecko

▶ Bringing your gecko home

▶ Setting up a schedule

● ●

*Y*ou have a lot to do before you bring home your new leopard gecko. You need a cage or enclosure and have to decide where to keep that cage. You also need to furnish the cage so your leopard gecko can be happy and thrive. Once all that is done, you have to get her home safely. So to make sure you don't miss anything important, I give you all the details you need in this chapter to make sure your gecko gets settled in safely and comfortably.

Creating the Perfect Cage

Too many new gecko owners buy their gecko and supplies at the same time. They bring her home in a little box and then leave her there while they set up the cage. Halfway through the set up, they realize something is broken or they're missing a vital part. Meanwhile, the leopard gecko is still in that cramped little box with no heat. The owner ends up frustrated, the lizard is cold and stressed, and it's a bad situation all the way around.

It's better for all — you and your new gecko — to set up the cage at least a day ahead of time. You can then make sure you have everything you need, and you can be sure that everything works as it should. To begin with, I've listed the supplies you'll need:

✔ One 10-gallon (40-liter) tank or an equivalent size cage for one leopard gecko; a 12- to 15-gallon-sized (45- to 60-liter-sized) cage for two. The tank must have a securely fitted screen top or doors.

✔ One reptile undertank heater.

✔ One ceramic heater.

- One light fixture for this cage top heater.
- Two reptile thermometers (the kind with adhesive that sticks to the sides of the tank are good).
- Water and food dishes (very shallow) or plastic jar lids.
- Substrate.
- Two hiding spots.
- Cage furnishings (silk plants, rocks, pieces of bark).

You will eventually need some more supplies (food, vitamins, and so forth), but we'll go over those in Chapter 5.

Comparing the different types of cages

The basic leopard gecko cage for first-time owners is usually a glass tank, like an aquarium, but one that doesn't necessarily hold water. Glass tanks for reptile use don't have to hold water, they just need to be glued enough to hold the pieces of glass together. Although the basic glass tanks work well for leopard geckos, they aren't necessarily the right tank or best tank for you or your geckos. Read the following sections to get an idea of what type of tank works best for you and your gecko.

A good cage keeps your lizard safe from outside threats, prevents your lizard from escaping, and keeps your lizard's food (crickets and other insects) from getting away.

Glass tanks

Glass tanks are inexpensive (a 10-gallon/40-liter tank can often be bought for less than $20) and are easy to find. These tanks are easy to wash out and clean (the small ones anyway) and can be furnished so they look nice. The downside is that glass breaks so they must be handled carefully when moved or when being cleaned.

When you buy a glass tank, don't forget you need a lid. If the tank doesn't come with a screen top, you can buy it separately at stores where reptile supplies are sold.

Leopard geckos can do well in glass tanks as long as they have several hiding spots. If there are no hiding spots, a leopard gecko in a glass tank will feel exposed and vulnerable and will begin to suffer from stress, which will eventually cause her health to suffer.

Plastic one-piece cages

I use commercially made, one-piece plastic cages, which are available from reptile specialty stores, via the Internet, or found through advertisements in reptile magazines. These cages are made of one piece of molded plastic with two sliding glass doors in the front. They're also stackable, so two, three or even four cages can be stacked on top of each other.

The solid sides, top, and bottom give the leopard gecko a feeling of security (nothing is going to sneak up on him!) yet the glass in the front allows you to watch your pet. I have also found that this style of cage cuts down on the number of crickets who escape from the gecko's cage — always a good thing!

Custom cages

Many cage manufacturers make custom reptile cages. These can be made out of stained wood, laminated materials, or plastic. The cages are usually very attractive — much more so than the simple glass tank or plain plastic cage.

If you want your leopard gecko's cage to be an attractive addition to your home, you may want to look into a custom cage, but I would advise you to wait a little while. Many people decide to change how their reptile pets are housed after having them for a little while. Keep your gecko a few months, care for her, clean her cage, and then you can decide what you may like to change.

Getting the right size

The minimum size tank for a single leopard gecko should be no smaller than the equivalent of a 10-gallon (40-liter) tank. These are made in different heights, widths, and lengths, but a tank that is 20 to 24 inches long by 14 to 16 inches wide (61 centimeters long by 36 to 41 centimeters wide) will be fine.

A leopard gecko, once established in her tank, will go to one corner to relieve herself. This makes cage cleaning much easier. However, if the cage is too small, the gecko won't have room to do this.

If you decide to get two, three, or four leopard geckos, plan on increasing the tank by 2.5 to 5 gallons (10 to 20 liters) per gecko. This will give each gecko room to move, get away from the others, and live comfortably.

Keeping the cage secure

Leopard geckos are not bad escape artists; some lizards are much worse. But once your gecko's free, she is tough to catch, and she may bite! Given the chance, even a tame leopard will crawl away to see the world. Therefore, keeping the cage secure is an important part of keeping your gecko safe.

Most glass tanks that are manufactured for reptile use come with a screen top that can be secured with a pin (much like a cotter pin). If the tank is second hand or if it was originally an aquarium, there are screen tops you can buy separately that can be fastened to the top of the tank with Velcro.

The one-piece plastic commercial cages have sliding glass doors in the front. These glass doors can be lifted out of their runners for cleaning but are too heavy for a leopard gecko to move. However, if you have children in the house who may decide to play with the gecko without your permission or supervision, you may want to buy locks for these sliding glass doors, available at most reptile supply stores.

Putting it in the right spot

Where you place the cage is very important. Follow these guidelines when choosing a location for your gecko's cage:

- Never put a cage where direct sun will hit it, even for just a few minutes a day. The cage can heat up very quickly, killing your leopard gecko.

- Don't put the cage in an unstable location. Many bookshelves, for example, may be very unsteady, causing the cage to come toppling down. A glass tank with substrate and cage furnishings can weigh several pounds, so make sure it's on a steady and stable foundation.

- Place the cage where it will be seen every day, hopefully, several times a day. If it's in an out-of-the-way location, it's too easy to forget about your gecko. She may go days without water or food, or her cage may get disgustingly dirty. When seen every day, it's much easier to remember her, feed and fill her water bowl, and handle her.

- Although you want to place the cage where it will be seen, you also don't want to put the cage where it will be constantly disturbed during the day when she's sleeping. (In Chapter 6,

I discuss in more detail what it's like to be nocturnal.) So you want to achieve a happy medium; close enough to be seen and cared for yet quiet enough to sleep undisturbed.

✔ Don't put the leopard gecko cage in the kitchen. To prevent any accidental transmission of disease or other health threats (to you or to your gecko), keep your pet away from any areas where food is handled, prepared, or eaten.

Cleaning the cage

No matter where you've bought your cage, you need to clean it well before you add anything to it, including your gecko. Follow these simple steps to get your cage sparkling clean:

1. **Scrub out the cage or tank, using a diluted bleach solution (do not use any other cleaners as most are toxic to reptiles).**

2. **Rinse it very, very well — all the bleach smell should be gone.**

3. **Dry the cage with a clean towel or paper towels.**

Turning Up the Heavenly Heat

Leopard geckos, like other reptiles, are cold-blooded. They do not produce heat internally through chemical reactions as mammals (who are warm-blooded) do. Instead, reptiles absorb heat from the sun directly (by basking in the sun) or by laying in a warm area or on a warm surface. The heat that is absorbed then allows the reptile's body to process food and perform the many other internal functions that mammals can do without external help.

Since leopard geckos are nocturnal and sleep during the day while the sun is out, they do not bask in the sun. Instead, they absorb heat from the ground that has been heated by the sun. This is very efficient for the species, since their native habitat (Afghanistan, Iran, Iraq, Pakistan and India) can be so very hot and dry. If these small lizards basked in direct sunlight, they would quickly dehydrate and overheat. However, since they sleep during the day in shelter under rocks or debris, they can avoid the worst of the heat and come out at night when the air is cooler but the ground is still warm. So it's important to provide and control the temperature in your gecko's cage.

Making temperature gradients

In the wild, reptiles move throughout their environment, not just to find food, but to regulate their body temperature. As the reptiles heat up, they move to a slightly cooler (but not cold) spot so that the heating process doesn't continue to increase. If the reptiles cool too much, they move to a warmer spot. This *thermoregulation* (the process of controlling the body's temperature) is ongoing and vital to the reptile's health, well-being, and survival.

In captivity, your leopard gecko needs to continue this thermoregulation. Therefore, when you provide heat for her cage, the heat should be supplied to one end or corner of the cage only. With one spot heated, she can then move between the heated spot and cooler, unheated sections of the cage to control her body heat. The temperature differences throughout the cage are called *temperature gradients*.

Never force your leopard gecko to remain in any temperature gradient; she knows best what she needs and will move back and forth on her own.

Determining heat requirements

Leopard geckos need heat to function, which in their native habitat is rarely a problem, but in captivity, you need to supply enough heat artificially so that one end of the cage (the hottest temperature gradient) reaches 80 to 85 degrees Fahrenheit (27 to 29 degrees Celsius). Even 90 degrees Fahrenheit (32 degrees Celsius) is okay. The hottest temperature gradient shouldn't be hotter than 90 degrees Fahrenheit (32 degrees Celsius) nor should it be cooler than 80 degrees Fahrenheit (27 degrees Celsius). Too hot and the lizard may dehydrate; too cool and the leopard gecko may not be able to digest her food. The coolest part of the cage (the coolest temperature gradient in the cage) during the day can fall to normal room temperatures.

If your local area is experiencing a severe heat wave and temperatures throughout your leopard gecko's cage rise to more than 90 degrees Fahrenheit (32 degrees Celsius), turn off all heat in the cage and make sure your leopard gecko has plenty of water. She can always lay close to or in the water to cool off.

Providing heat

Heat can be provided in many different ways. Some will come naturally from the heat in your house. Summer weather is normally warmer during the day and cooler at night, both of which are good for your gecko, and during the winter, most of us heat our homes during the day. Unfortunately, however, few of us keep our homes as consistently as warm (well, hot!) as the gecko needs in one section of her cage.

You can find several products that can increase the heat in the leopard gecko's cage. They include:

✔ **Undertank heaters:** Undertank (or undercage) heat pads or heat tapes are excellent for heating leopard gecko cages. These are either rubber pads with heating elements inside, or plastic tapes with heating elements inside. Both are fastened under the tank or cage at one end (to provide a temperature gradient) and then plugged into an electrical source (see Figure 4-1). Because the heat will then be coming from underneath, your gecko can hide during the day to sleep, as she would normally, and the substrate under her will be warm.

Not only are undertank heaters more natural for leopard geckos (with the heat coming from below), but these heaters also use less energy than do incandescent lights, so they save on your electrical bill.

Read and follow the directions for your undercage heater. Most of them require some air space between the heater and the surface where the cage is sitting (such as a wooden shelf) so that the shelf won't overheat. Usually a wooden or plastic shim is all that's needed; just something to slightly elevate the cage so that heat can escape.

Buying the right size of undertank heater is crucial — the undertank heater should take up no more than one-third of the total floor space of the cage. If you buy one that is too large, your leopard gecko won't be able to get far enough away from it when she needs to cool down.

✔ **Heat rocks:** Heat rocks (also called hot rocks) were one of the first means available for nocturnal reptile owners to provide heat from below the cage. A heat rock is a rock (ceramic, stone, or concrete) with a heating element inside. Although early models simply produced heat with no adjustments, today, many are adjustable.

Because many reptiles lay directly on them and would burn their bellies or feet before they moved, reptile owners shy away from heat rocks. However, these heating tools can be used quite efficiently if they are buried in the substrate so that the heat comes from below as it does from heat tapes. If the heat rock is a newer model that is adjustable, that's even better. You can bury it, and then monitor the temperature so it doesn't get too hot.

Figure 4-1: An undertank heater should be placed under one end of the tank only so that it can provide a temperature gradient.

✔ **Ceramic heaters:** Ceramic heaters screw into an incandescent light bulb socket and produce heat without producing light. Because the heat from these comes from above (as it does with incandescent light bulbs) these are not the best way to produce all the heat your gecko needs. However, they can be used for supplemental heat when the room temperature is chilly. For example, during the winter, your home may be cool especially at night, and some extra heat may be needed to keep your leopard gecko's cage from getting too cold. A ceramic heater can provide some extra heat without providing the light that an incandescent light would put out.

Ceramic heaters come in different sizes just as incandescent light bulbs do. For a 10-gallon (40-liter) tank, a 40-watt heater works well. If your house is quite chilly in the winter (or if the air conditioner is on full force during the summer), you may want to use a 60-watt heater.

Like incandescent lights, you should place ceramic heaters above the cage and securely fasten them. You can cause a fire if the heater — placed outside of the cage or not fastened securely — gets knocked to the floor or brushed aside into the drapes.

✔ **Incandescent light bulbs:** Incandescent light bulbs produce heat, with the higher wattage bulbs producing more heat than the bulbs with less wattage. For many years, reptile enthusiasts have used incandescent bulbs to heat reptile tanks because they felt a bright bulb located above the cage would duplicate the sun. The light and heat will come from above, and the reptile can bask in the heat.

You must place incandescent lights above the cage and fasten them securely. Many fires have started because the lights were knocked to the floor or brushed aside into the drapes.

Although incandescent does work for some reptiles, it doesn't work as well for leopard geckos. Leopard geckos, being nocturnal, do not bask in the sun to increase their body temperature. So the light from above is wasted. In addition, incandescent light bulbs use a lot of energy and will therefore, increase your energy bill, especially if you decide to increase your leopard gecko population and set up several tanks.

On the other hand, incandescent lights do allow you to see what's going on in the cage. You can set up an incandescent light (lower wattage — perhaps 25 to 40 watts) with a screw-in light bulb socket and a reflective hood above the cage.

Never leave an incandescent light on above your leopard gecko's cage at night; leopard geckos are nocturnal, and a white light would disrupt your gecko's activities, especially eating.

Monitoring the temperature

Now that you have heat going into the tank, you must monitor it a few times a day while the cage is new and the heater is getting warm, then once a day for as long as the cage has inhabitants. You need two thermometers — one for the hottest spot and one for the coolest spot in the cage — so you can check on the temperature in the cage. Use thermometers that stick on the side of the cage and face front so you can see them easily.

You want the hot temperature gradient (the hottest spot in the cage) to be between 85 degrees Fahrenheit (29 degrees Celsius) and 90 degrees Fahrenheit (32 degrees Celsius). So place a thermometer in that spot. If the cage is not warm enough, you may have to get a larger undertank heater or add a ceramic heater on top of the cage. Place another thermometer in the coolest spot in the cage. If the cooler temperature gradient is not significantly cooler (at least 75 degrees Fahrenheit/24 degrees Celsius) move the heater (heat rock, heat tape and ceramic heater) farther toward one end or one corner. Make sure it's not in the center of that cage or covering the entire cage.

You want your leopard gecko to be able to move around to regulate her body temperature. If the entire cage is warm, she may overheat or dehydrate. If the cool end of the cage is too cool, the gecko may get chilled and may slow down too much to move back to a warmer spot.

Don't have the cage in an entertainment center or above electronics; they produce heat, too, and can keep the cage uncontrollably hot.

Once your gecko's tank is set up and the heater (undertank, heat rock, or ceramic) is plugged in to an electrical source, check it often the first few days. It takes at least an hour for most heaters to reach full heat output (depending upon the make and brand) and then it takes a while for the substrate to warm up. Keep checking the thermometers (several times a day for the first two or three days) to make sure the tank is warm enough in its hot temperature gradient and isn't too warm where it should be cooler.

Furnishing Your Gecko's Home

If you have your cage set up and your heater plugged in (see earlier in the chapter if you don't), you need to put something in the bottom of the tank (the substrate), and you need to furnish the tank. A bare tank would be easy to clean, but this wouldn't be at all comfortable for your gecko.

Digging in the dirt (or sand)

The *substrate* is the material on the floor of the cage. This is also called *bedding*. The substrate you use should be easy to clean, comfortable for your gecko, and safe. Check out the following choices:

- ✔ **Wood shavings:** Wood shavings, although inexpensive, light-weight when cleaning, and easy-to-find at any pet supply store, aren't a natural substrate for leopard geckos. When damped by spilled water, they stay damp — too damp for a desert animal. In addition, pine and cedar shavings should be avoided entirely as they have tree oils that can be dangerous for your gecko. Shavings other than pine or cedar can be used for short-term use if nothing else is available (a day or two) but should not be used as regular bedding.

✓ **Alfalfa pellets and other agricultural products:** Many reptile owners who keep herbivorous reptiles use alfalfa pellets (rabbit food) as bedding. That way, if the lizard eats any of the bedding, it itself can be good food. This is great for baby tortoises but not good for leopard geckos. Not only are leopard geckos not herbivores, but again, like wood shavings, if the pellets get wet, they stay wet. They can get moldy and create a bad living environment for your gecko.

You can find substrates made from a variety of agricultural products, including corncobs. The corncob beddings do not seem to stay as wet like wood shavings and alfalfa pellets do, but they still get moldy once water has spilled on them. I would use them in an emergency situation only.

✓ **Walnut and other hard wood beddings:** Some of the new reptile beddings include some made from walnut shells and other hardwoods. The beddings almost seem like sand but are coarser in texture. In the cage, these are very attractive and have a more natural appearance than do wood shavings or corncob pellets. In addition, when wet, these beddings do not seem to get as moldy as the previously mentioned beddings do. These beddings are not inexpensive, however. Your cage will be heavier with beddings such as these, and you will need to make sure the stand or support under the cage can hold it.

✓ **Sand:** The terrain where leopard geckos originated varies from rocky almost mountainous deserts to lower, sandier deserts. Clay-gravel soil with rocks of various sizes and blown sand are very common. Obviously we cannot duplicate that in a cage, but by using sand in the cage, we can come pretty close.

Sand box sand, the kind bought for a child's sand box, is silica sand and has sharp edges. Over time this can cause abrasions on the leopard gecko's skin and can potentially cause an intestinal blockage if very small, young geckos picked up some sand with their food and swallowed it. However, several companies have packaged and marketed calcium sands that have smaller rounded grains that are not supposed to be as harmful to the skin and less dangerous when swallowed.

Sand is heavy so make sure the supports under your gecko's cage can hold the weight. When cleaning the cage, scoop the sand out, don't try to lift the cage with the sand in it; the bottom can drop out.

Baby geckos should not be housed on sand, even calcium sand, because the long-term safety is not known. An intestinal impaction is a very real possibility. Use paper towels (see below) instead.

✔ **Paper towels and newspapers:** Paper towels are the most inexpensive bedding you can use and probably the ugliest, too. Even the decorator ones! However, most leopard gecko breeders house their newly hatched geckos on paper towels because they are inexpensive, very safe, and easy to clean from the cage. For babies, paper towels are the best choice. For adults, it makes for a very unattractive cage.

Newspapers are also used quite often, again, because they are easily available and cheap. I do have some concerns about the inks used on many newspapers. They are supposed to be safe, but I know of no long-term studies showing the safety of the ink in regards to reptiles. I would use newspapers with caution and only for short-term use (for a day or two).

Recycled newspaper beddings are manufactured for use with reptiles and other small animals. They are lightweight, absorbent, and completely safe. They do not get moldy and are dust free. The drawbacks are the price (they are not cheap), and they have a musty odor, which some people find objectionable. Also, they tend to be unattractive. (They are gray and look like crumpled, shredded paper.)

Hiding spots

Hiding spots are exactly that: Places you provide for your leopard gecko where she can hide away from potential dangers and sleep. Without a hiding spot, your gecko feels exposed and vulnerable, which causes stress to build up that compromises her health. It's best to have two hiding spots: one in the hottest temperature gradient and one in the coolest.

The hiding spots can be as simple as a small cardboard box with a door cut out of it or as elaborate as a commercially made plastic or ceramic reptile hideout. Most reptile supply stores (or stores that carry reptiles) also sell pieces of cork bark. These have a curve in them where the bark fit against the tree, making them excellent hiding spots.

Make sure any hiding spot you use is clean and is safe for the lizard (no cleansers or soap residues, pesticides, or herbicides). When you put the hiding spot in the cage, make sure it's secure and won't fall down and crush the gecko.

If you want to put a couple of things together to make a hiding spot (such as several flat stones or a couple pieces of bark) you can use silicone aquarium glue. Once it's cured, it's safe to use around reptiles.

Choosing additional furnishings

You can make your gecko's cage look more home-like by adding a few rocks, a couple small pieces of bark, or even a few silk flowers. You can even add a few fake desert plants to make it look like a real desert. Many reptile supply stores also carry reptile cage backgrounds. One of these, sized to fit your leopard gecko's cage, will add an attractive sense of realism. These furnishing are for your benefit; your gecko doesn't need them, but they do make the cage more attractive.

Some leopard gecko keepers have even experimented with using live desert plants. I recommend not using cactus with spines (to protect yourself and your gecko). It usually works best if you have several plants, rotating them in the cage a week at a time. Otherwise the plants die quickly because they don't have adequate light in the cage.

No matter what you put in the cage to make it look homey for your gecko, just make sure the furnishings are clean and safe, and leave enough floor space in the cage for your gecko to move around. Remember, you want the cage to look nice, but it's also your gecko's home.

The cage furnishings should also be easy to keep clean (see Figure 4-1). You will be setting up a regular cleaning schedule for this cage; if it's too difficult to keep clean, you will end up stripping the cage — taking everything out of it — or you won't clean it as often as you should. So as you set up the cage, keep cleaning in mind.

Getting Your Gecko Safely Home

If you set up the cage and turned on and stabilized the heat, you're ready to bring home your new pet. If you're ordering her via the Internet, this is the time to have her shipped to your door. If you're picking her up from the breeder or store, now you need to go get her.

Traveling safely

If your gecko is being shipped to you, the seller can give you guidance as to which company ships reptiles safely (there aren't many that ship reptiles at all!) and how to go about it. The seller will also be keeping an eye on the weather; they won't ship reptiles when it's too hot or too cold. If they tell you that they are going to wait for the weather to change, don't argue. Breeders or distributors who ship reptiles often know best. It's best to wait and have your gecko arrive safely than argue and have a dead gecko in the package. Make sure that when the gecko is shipped, you're going to be at home to receive the package. Unpack it right away, and then let the seller know (via phone or e-mail) that your gecko has arrived safely.

If you plan on picking your gecko up yourself, keep the following in mind so your gecko gets home safely:

- ✔ **Bring a small carry cage with you to the store or plan on buying one there.** Most pet store or reptile stores will send a small reptile home in a small box or a deli-type plastic cup.

  The small reptile carrying cages are like the equivalent of a small cat carrier. They can be used later to hold your gecko while you're cleaning her cage.

- ✔ **Watch the weather.** If the weather is very hot, make sure your gecko is riding home in your car with the air conditioning on low (not high! don't freeze him!). Don't let her carrying cage sit where the sun will shine on it; that cage (or the store's box or deli cup) will overheat rapidly.

  If the weather is very cold, warm up your car before you bring her out of the store, or carry her in her container carefully inside your coat until the car heats up. Leopard geckos do not tolerate cold well at all, so bringing your gecko home in the middle of winter in a cold climate should be undertaken with care and planning.

- ✔ **Do not open your gecko's cage on the way home.** Don't peek at her, check on her, or bask in her beauty. Keep her cage or box securely closed until you get home. She's going to be upset at traveling anyway, and when you open that cage or box, you may be surprised at how fast an upset gecko can move. Keep her safe; keep her caged.

Getting your gecko used to her new home

After you get home with your new gecko (remember, your cage should already be set up and heated — see earlier in this chapter for more on setting up and heating the cage) open her carrying cage, gently lift her out, and set her in her new home. Give her a few days to settle in before you begin handling her. It's going to take her a while to explore her new home and decide where she wants to sleep, eat, and defecate. So give her some time.

Don't invite your neighbors, friends and family over to see your new pet. As I said, give her time to settle in and time to get to know you. Later, in a few weeks, as people come over for other reasons, you can show off your leopard gecko.

Keeping Up with the Housekeeping

The cage is set up, your leopard gecko is at home, and now the work begins — or at least as soon as your leopard gecko makes her first mess. Housekeeping (or cage cleaning) is one of those ongoing chores that never ends as long as you keep your leopard gecko.

Carrying out daily chores

The daily chores are not difficult; they just take some time to do and some self-discipline to make sure you do them. Once your gecko is in her new cage, you need to take a look at your daily schedule, decide when you can spare 15 to 20 minutes each and every day for gecko chores, And then set aside this time.

Your daily gecko chores include:

- Remove the food saucer, wash it, and dry it.
- Put the food saucer back in the cage with fresh food. (I discuss food in Chapter 5.)
- Remove the water saucer, wash it, refill it, and put it back in the cage.
- Remove any dead, uneaten insects.
- Scoop out any feces with a spoon dedicated for this purpose or a cat litter scoop.
- Pick up the gecko, look her over, and make sure all is well. (See Chapter 7 for more on healthy geckos.)

Cleaning the cage weekly

Once a week you need to clean the cage, which isn't hard to do. As with the daily chores (see above), it just takes some time. If you follow these steps, you'll not only have a clean cage, but also a happy, healthy gecko:

1. **Take your gecko out of her cage, and put her in her carrying cage.**

2. **Unplug the undercage heater, the ceramic heater, and/or fluorescent light. Set them aside.**

3. **Take the food and water saucers out of the cage and wash them.**

4. **Take all the furnishings out of the cage and wash them well with a diluted bleach solution (do not use any other cleaners as most are toxic to reptiles). If the sun's shining, set them out in the sun to dry and disinfect.**

5. **Scoop the substrate out of the cage, dispose of it in a plastic trash bag, and throw it away.**

6. **Wash the cage using a diluted bleach solution, scrub it well, and then rinse until the bleach smell is gone.**

7. **Dry the cage with a clean towel or paper towels.**

8. **Once the outside of the cage is dry, plug the undercage heater back in.**

9. **When the inside of the cage is dry, add your new substrate.**

10. **Set up the cage furnishings again, keeping the bowls and hiding spots in the same places, but rearranging any other furnishings if you want to.**

11. **Put the food and water saucers back in the cage with fresh food and water.**

12. **Put the top back on the cage or close the doors.**

13. **Put the ceramic heater and fluorescent light back on top if you're using them.**

14. **Put your leopard gecko back in her cage.**

After you get the hang of it, cleaning won't take long. I can clean a cage following these directions in less than a half hour — with practice so can you.

Chapter 5

Caring for Your Leopard Gecko

*C*aptive leopard geckos should, with good care, live at least 20 years, but your leopard gecko can't do that alone; he needs your help. He needs good nutritious foods, vitamin and mineral supplements, and the occasional treat, of course. Since it won't rain inside his cage, he also needs clean fresh water provided in a way so that he can find it, and he needs some stimulation so that he gets some exercise. Obviously, geckos have needs, but, in this chapter, I explain exactly how to provide good loving care for your gecko without making you feel like your entire life is spent waiting on your gecko hand and foot, er, claw and claw.

Feeding the Hungry Beast

In the wild, leopard geckos eat just about any moving insect that they can catch that fits in their mouths. They have been known to eat spiders, hard-shelled beetles, and beetle larvae. Some experts say that leopard geckos will even eat scorpions! Of course, in captivity you will not be risking your gecko's life by feeding scorpions to him, but as an *insectivore* (one that eats insects) he needs to be fed live insects as his primary diet. In the following sections, I discuss how to prepare (and even raise) a healthy diet for your gecko.

Discovering crickets

Crickets make a good meal for your leopard gecko if, and only if, the crickets themselves are well fed (see Figure 5-1). Crickets commercially raised for reptiles are well fed, but during transportation to pet stores and often at the stores themselves, they are not fed. So, it's important that leopard gecko owners feed their crickets well before feeding them to the leopard gecko. If not, the cricket will be nothing more than an empty shell and will provide no nutrition at all to the reptile. Feeding the crickets prior to feeding them to your gecko is called *gut loading* because what the cricket is fed is what your gecko then gets. (See the section later on feeding and caring for crickets for more information on feeding them.)

Figure 5-1: Well-fed crickets are good food for your gecko.

How many crickets your leopard gecko eats depends entirely upon him: his age, his size, his activity level, and his appetite. You just have to feed him and watch how many he eats.

When you feed crickets to your leopard gecko, take five or six crickets and drop them into your gecko's cage. Don't add any more than that at any one time because the crickets, surviving in the cage, will not be eating well themselves, so when your gecko eats them, they will no longer be good food. Plus, hungry crickets can torment your gecko, even to the point of biting him! When the first five or six are gone, drop in a couple more.

Caring for crickets

You can buy as many crickets as you want or need at most pet stores. You can go in daily and buy one cricket if you want, or you can go in once a week and get a couple dozen. If you buy crickets in small amounts, they are usually 8¢ to 10¢ each. If you buy them in bulk and keep them for a while, they are significantly cheaper.

If you buy crickets in bulk (500 to 1,000), you can then keep them for several weeks, feeding them, and giving them to your leopard gecko as he needs them. Some crickets may die in the process (they are very short lived), but the others will be good food for your lizard. To keep crickets, you need to set up another tank. You just need to get the following supplies:

- A glass tank (the bigger the better since crickets can jump) The tank doesn't have to be huge, a 15-gallon (60-liter) tank is fine, but taller is better than long and shallow.

- A very secure, tight screen top for the tank

- Plain, unflavored, uncooked (dry) oatmeal; the quick cooking kind is fine but do not use the flavored oatmeal with fruit and sugar — that will draw ants!

- Carrots

- Cardboard egg crates

- Jar lid

- Sponge

To set up the tank for your crickets, you must:

1. **Clean the tank.** Scrub out the tank and rinse it well, making sure there is no soap or bleach residue. Dry it well.

2. **Put oatmeal in the tank.** Take the plain, unflavored, uncooked oatmeal and spread an inch-deep layer on the bottom of the tank. The oatmeal serves as both substrate and food for the crickets.

3. **Put carrots in the tank.** Take two or three carrots and chop them up into one-inch sections, then scatter them over the floor of the tank on top of the oatmeal. These provide moisture for the crickets as well as added nutrition.

4. **Put egg crates in the tank.** If you buy crickets in bulk, they will be in boxes with several *egg crates* (the egg-shaped cardboard that keeps eggs stable). The egg crates keep the crickets from crushing each other and gives them something to climb on and hide under. Tear up a couple of these into 6-inch sections and drop them into the tank.

5. **Put water in the tank.** Crickets will drown in open water so you need to provide water with a sponge. Take the sponge and cut it with scissors to fit the jar lid. Set it into the jar lid, and then moisten it. The excess water will be caught by the jar lid. Set this in the tank.

6. **Put the crickets in the tank.** Just dump them into the tank. Don't worry about being gentle; just dump them in. Do it quickly because if you hesitate, you'll have escapees!

To catch crickets to feed your leopard gecko, put a small steep-sided bowl on the floor of the cricket tank. Pick up one of the pieces of egg crate and shake it on top of the bowl. (This is why you wanted small pieces of egg crate instead of big ones.) When you have enough crickets, just pick up the bowl, cover it with your hand, and take it to your gecko.

You can find crickets farms on the Internet and in the list in Chapter 8.

Raising crickets

Many people who keep several (or many) reptiles raise their own crickets. When you raise your own, you can have on hand crickets of various sizes to feed reptiles of various sizes (baby geckos eat tiny crickets). In addition, you know what kind of nutrition your geckos are getting because you have the crickets.

Set up a tank like you did for feeding the crickets except put a two-inch layer of sand in the bottom instead of oatmeal. The females lay their eggs in this sand. Then provide oatmeal in a flat saucer or two. Drop in two or three dozen adult crickets.

If the weather is warm, the crickets are okay just like this. If it's cool (less than 70 degrees Fahrenheit/21 degrees Celsius), put a ceramic heater (or an incandescent light) above the cage.

After a couple of weeks, catch the adult crickets and move them to another tank. You can feed them to your leopard gecko, or put them in another breeding tank. In the now vacant tank where the adult crickets used to be, watch for the baby crickets. They will appear as teeny tiny little bugs crawling around the cage. They hide a lot so will be found under the egg crates. Keep providing food, carrots and water in the sponge and watch them grow.

Making a meal of mealworms

Mealworms make a good meal for many species, including birds, primates, and mammals, as well as reptiles. Mealworms, like crickets, should be fed prior to being fed to your gecko because they may not have been well fed during transportation. In addition, most mealworms are kept refrigerated prior to their sale at the pet store, and they do not eat while refrigerated.

Feed your leopard gecko six to eight mealworms at a time, putting the mealworms in a shallow reptile dish or a plastic jar lid. If the mealworms are simply dropped into the cage, they will dig into the substrate and disappear. Once the initial offer of mealworms has been eaten, you can offer a few more mealworms but add just a few at a time.

Feeding mealworms

As with crickets, you can buy mealworms in small amounts (25, 50, or 100 to a deli cup) or you can buy them in bulk. No matter what size you get, you should always feed them prior to giving them to your gecko.

To feed just a few mealworms, set up a small plastic container and put some wheat bran, oat bran, or cornmeal in the bottom. A quarter inch over the bottom is fine. Grate a carrot and drop the pieces over the top of the bran. Drop in your mealworms, let them eat, and over the next few days, feed them to your geckos.

Raising mealworms

You can raise your own mealworms; it's not difficult. Set up a glass tank, again one with a screen top. Put a layer of about 2 inches (5 centimeters) of wheat or oat bran on the bottom as both substrate and food. Chop up some carrots and drop them on the bedding. The mealworms will burrow into the bedding. Dump in 100 mealworms and replenish the carrots as the old ones disappear or dry up. Add some more bran every once in a while.

You will see pupa on the top of the bedding first. Later, in a few weeks, you will begin to see some dark brown or black beetles. And eventually, when you sift through the bran, you will begin to see some very small mealworms. Ah, the circle of life!

Never dump out bedding or wastes that may contain insects in your compost heap. The eggs, larva, pupa, or insects can survive and become pests, potentially causing a major problem in your house, yard, and the environment. Always dispose of wastes in a plastic trash bag.

Meeting waxworms

Waxworms are the soft bodied, white- to cream-colored larva for a moth. They are high in fat and very nutritious for fast growing young leopard geckos or for breeding adults. Because they are high in fat, they can also cause an adult leopard gecko to become obese if he eats too many of them. Waxworms, then, should be a part of a good diet but should never be the only insect fed to leopard geckos.

Waxworms are also very difficult to raise so they will not be a project for your garage. Instead, you will need to buy them as you need them. Prior to feeding them to your gecko, keep waxworms in the refrigerator. If not refrigerated, they may turn into pupa and then moths, or if they get too warm, they will die.

Offer waxworms six to eight at a time in a small, shallow, reptile feeding dish or in a plastic jar lid (see Figure 5-2). As with mealworms, if you don't put them into a dish of some sort, they will rapidly burrow into the substrate and disappear. Don't feed your gecko more than six to eight waxworms at any one feeding as these insects are very fattening.

Figure 5-2: Provide waxworms in a shallow dish or saucer to slow down escapes.

Creating a varied diet

In a natural situation, an insectivore will eat anything edible that it can catch. This variety keeps the insectivore healthy. In captivity, we can serve our leopard geckos best by doing the same thing. Although a gecko may remain healthy eating just mealworms (well-fed mealworms that is), providing a varied diet is more natural, reduces the chances of nutritional deficiencies, and improves your gecko's overall mental and physical health by sparking his interest in hunting and giving him some exercise.

You can vary your gecko's diet by alternating crickets, mealworms, and waxworms, but you can also add some other insects to the diet. If your backyard is clean (no insecticides), use a net to scoop some insects from the grass. Catch a few sowbugs (pillbugs) and some small earthworms. These "wild" insects add nutritional variety and get your leopard gecko excited about hunting.

Adding vitamins and minerals

When fed a varied diet, leopard geckos generally thrive. However, because not all insect diets are equal, the geckos should be fed a vitamin and mineral supplement. Baby geckos, especially while growing so rapidly, and breeding adult geckos also need this extra nutrition.

Calcium

All geckos should have access to calcium in the form of calcium carbonate or calcium gluconate (found in pet supply stores). Once a week, this can be dusted on crickets prior to feeding them to your gecko. Put a half a teaspoon of the powdered calcium in a plastic bag. Drop in six crickets, inflate the bag and shake gently. Drop the dusted crickets in the gecko's cage. As the gecko eats, he'll also get his calcium.

Calcium can also be offered in a shallow reptile dish or a small jar lid. Simply place a small spoonful of the calcium in the dish and set it in the cage. Your gecko will discover it, and as he needs it, will lick it up. Pregnant females and growing babies have a continuing need for calcium.

Rapidly growing baby leopard geckos without an adequate source of calcium may develop metabolic bone disease, leading to their death.

Vitamin/mineral combination

Once a week you can dust the crickets with a reptile vitamin/mineral supplement. (Don't do this at the same time you dust with calcium but do it another day.) There are several vitamin/mineral formulas on the market. Just choose one that is specifically for lizards.

Many of these vitamin/mineral supplements recommend using it every day. If the insects you feed your gecko are themselves well fed, and if you are offering your gecko a varied diet, adding vitamins and minerals every day is not needed. Once a week for healthy adults is fine. You can offer it twice a week for babies and for breeding females.

Feeding commercial foods

There are a variety of commercial foods available now for reptiles, including leopard geckos. Some of these include canned dead insects (crickets, mealworms, and flies) with vitamins added. There are also formulated foods that come canned, dry, pelleted, and powdered. All kinds of different things are now for sale. However, just because these things are offered for sale doesn't mean your gecko recognizes them as food!

Keep in mind leopard geckos are stimulated by movement. A cricket hops, the gecko sees the movement and looks. The cricket moves again, and the gecko begins stalking. One more hop and the cricket is lunch. Canned dead insects don't move; therefore to the gecko, they are not food. If the gecko finds them by accident and investigates with his tongue, he may actually try one and eat it, and that's great. Just don't count on your gecko eating these and only these foods; make sure you have live insects available.

You can find commercial foods for feeding crickets and mealworms prior to giving them to reptiles, and these foods work very well. Since crickets and mealworms eat anything available, the new foods can be put into the insects' tank right away. This makes gut loading much easier. You can find these foods at any pet store with a reptile section.

Offering special treats

Most pet owners enjoy spoiling their pets once in a while. Cat owners give their cats catnip, and dog owners bring home a good rawhide. Leopard geckos can be spoiled once in a while, too, and your leopard gecko will enjoy it as much as you do!

A different (but of course, non-poisonous) insect from the backyard is always good. A spider (not a dangerous one), a hairless caterpillar, a small earthworm, a few sowbugs (pillbugs), or a small snail or slug are all good treats. As you try different insects from the backyard, pay attention to those insects that are eaten right away and those insects that are not. Always remove any uneaten insects after an hour or so. Your gecko obviously isn't hungry for those.

Adult leopard geckos will often eat a small baby mouse (called a *pinkie* because it hasn't yet grown hair). Although this bothers some people, it is natural. Any insectivorous or carnivorous reptile in the wild who finds a nest of mice will eat whatever he can swallow. Mice are on the menu! A pinkie mouse can be a special treat as well as good nutrition. You can buy pinkie mice at your reptile pet store.

If your leopard gecko will eat any of the commercial foods, offer those as treats once in a while. Some of my leopard geckos like the canned dead flies. There's something about the smell of them, I guess. It took a while for the geckos to catch on to the fact that these things were edible, but once they did, the flies were readily eaten.

You can teach your gecko to eat from your fingers by offering a very well liked food — such as waxworms — from your fingers only.

Providing Water

Many lizards get their water from rainfall, but leopard geckos, as true desert reptiles, get their water in an entirely different way. Leopard geckos take refuge under things during the day. In the wild, they may hide under rocks, overhanging ledges, or under debris. During the heating of the day and cooling of the night, any water moisture found in that spot will condense under the rock, ledge, or debris. The gecko then laps up that moisture one tiny droplet at a time. Leopard geckos look down for moisture, not up.

When you provide drinking water for your gecko, you need to provide it in a way that satisfies this need to find it low. Water should be in a very shallow reptile bowl or in a shallow plastic jar lid. That bowl or jar lid should then be set deep in the cage's substrate. Not so deep that the substrate will fall into the bowl and soil the water, but deep enough so that the leopard gecko can easily walk up to the water.

If the water is provided in a bowl that is too deep, the leopard gecko will not find it and will not drink. If the gecko is placed in the water (so that he finds it), he will panic and thrash out of it because to a gecko, deep water is dangerous. He still will not drink.

Keeping Your Gecko In Shape

Obesity is a problem with many captive reptiles, including leopard geckos, just as it is with people. When too much food is too readily available, it's easy to get fat. However, obesity is a health threat and can lead to a much shorter life.

All healthy adult leopard geckos should have a fat tail, and a fat tail doesn't necessarily mean the lizard is obese. However, when the tail assumes a more rounded shape, rather than a long fat shape, well, then the gecko may be approaching obesity. Healthy leopard geckos will have a curved body and some fat deposits behind the front legs. That's normal. However, if the tail is almost round, or the body is round, or if your gecko never wants to move except to eat; then he's probably obese. If your gecko stands up and his tummy is still dragging on the ground, that's obese.

Watching the diet

Varying your leopard gecko's diet will help prevent obesity. After all, crickets are not served to your gecko in a dish (as mealworms are); he must hunt and catch those crickets. That's good exercise. When you feed your obese gecko, just put a couple of crickets in the cage at a time. This way your gecko must try harder to catch them; if too many are dropped in at the same time, there is always a cricket within easy reach. When those two crickets are gone, then two more can be dropped in.

Waxworms are a good treat and excellent nutrition but should not be a large part of your gecko's diet because they are very high in fat. Because mealworms are good food and not overly high in fat, they can be a larger portion of the diet.

Keep track of how much your gecko eats. If he gets too fat, cut back slightly by feeding fewer insects. If he's too slim, add a few more. By making notes of how much your gecko eats and how often, you can better control the situation.

Encouraging exercise

You can't take your leopard gecko jogging with you nor can you expect him to run on an exercise wheel made for mice. But you can encourage him to move around more, which to a leopard gecko, is exercise.

The easiest way to encourage movement is to keep the cage interesting. Keep your gecko's food and water saucers in their normal place, and don't change the hiding spots (those are important to your gecko's sense of stability), but you can change the following, provided you make the changes one at a time:

- ✔ Bring in some different small rocks and stones. Set them around the cage (safely — you don't want them to fall and crush your gecko) and let him investigate them.

- ✔ Put a few pieces of different kinds of tree bark in the cage.

- ✔ Save a few toilet-paper cardboard tubes and pile them in the cage.

✔ Put one paper-towel cardboard tube in the cage.

✔ Bring in a handful of tree and weed leaves and pile them in an open section of the cage. Your gecko won't eat them but will sniff them and crawl through them.

Keep in mind your leopard gecko is nocturnal so make these changes in the evening and watch him as his cage and the room gets dark. He'll be very curious and will get exercise checking out these new things.

When making changes, do so one thing at a time and have a few days of normal routine before you add anything new. Remember your gecko's cage is his home, his place of security. Make changes to keep him active, but don't stress him out in the process.

Keeping Your Gecko Safe

Leopard geckos are sturdy little lizards, but they are still very small. It's very easy for them to get hurt, sometimes fatally, so it's up to you to keep your gecko safe from harm.

Keeping a cover on the cage

Make sure you keep a cover on your leopard gecko's cage. Although most adult leopard geckos do not have the ability to walk up glass walls (like tokay geckos can, for example) some of them can be quite determined and agile. I have a female leopard gecko who will wedge herself in a corner of a cage, and shimmy herself upwards. Luckily, she's in a one-piece plastic cage; if she was in a glass tank she may have gotten herself to the top already.

Be careful with baby geckos because they can walk up cage walls. Mother Nature has given them this ability as a means to escape danger, and they can do this for as long as a few months after hatching.

A tightly fitted, securely fastened screen top will keep your leopard gecko inside his cage where he belongs. It will also keep cricket escapes to a minimum!

A secure top to the cage will also keep other dangers out of the cage, especially dogs, cats, ferrets, birds, and little children's fingers — all things that can be a danger to a small gecko.

Socializing is not good

Other than their interaction with each other, and with you and your family, leopard geckos need not socialize. Do not force interactions with other pets. Other reptiles can be dangerous because they may carry *symbiotic* viruses, germs, or bacteria that coexist with them but may be dangerous to your leopard gecko. And vice versa. Dogs, cats, ferrets, and many other pets are by nature predators, and your leopard gecko can be seen as a tiny toy or worse yet, a snack.

Too much socialization with other people is not good, either. If you want to show your pet to friends, neighbors, or family, let them look at your gecko in his cage. Or you hold him as other people look at him. Let them rub his head gently. Too many people holding him is incredibly stressful for your gecko.

Preventing disasters

It's very difficult to love a pet and then lose him. That loss can come from the pet escaping or through death. Either one is very tough. However, many accidents with pets can be prevented. Just keep the following considerations in mind:

- ✔ Whenever you plan on taking your gecko out of his cage, put the dogs and cats away in another room with the door closed. Put a note on the door so other people in the house won't let them out.

- ✔ Keep the cage top securely closed. Use something to keep it closed so it won't accidentally slide open.

- ✔ Make sure the cage is set on a secure base. The shelf, table, or stand should not be wobbly. It needs to be able to carry the weight of the cage with all its furnishings.

- ✔ When cleaning the cage, put your gecko in his traveling cage and securely close the lid. Do not clean the cage with your gecko riding on your shoulder.

- ✔ When you take your gecko outside, put him in his traveling cage. Do not carry him outside in your hands.

Chapter 6

Getting to Know Your Gecko

In This Chapter
▶ Understanding leopard gecko behavior and communication
▶ Handling your gecko
▶ Making baby leopard geckos

L eopard geckos evolved for millions of years to become the creatures they are today. We've kept the species in captivity for several decades, but in comparison to the time the species has been in existence, that's nothing. So the leopard geckos we have today are creatures well able to survive in the wild; a harsh unforgiving environment. When we understand why geckos do what they do, especially in regards to their native habitat, we can then appreciate them more as pets in our home — you may even appreciate them enough to add more to your home and watch them create their own population explosion. In this chapter, I discuss the "whys" of your gecko's behavior and explain how to handle her properly. And for those of you interested in breeding, I get you started on the road to a houseful of geckos.

Understanding Leopard Gecko Behavior

Captive-bred leopard geckos may have never felt the sands of Afghanistan or seen a predatory fox, but their behaviors are still the same as they would be in the wild. Leopard geckos haven't been bred in captivity long enough to lose their wild instincts, reactions, and behaviors. So even though your leopard gecko may be a bit more relaxed than a wild-caught leopard, her behavior is still very natural.

Protecting themselves from predators

Leopard geckos originated in areas of Afghanistan, into Iran and Iraq, and portions of Pakistan and India. Many regions are harsh, unforgiving deserts, some were steppes at slightly higher elevations, and others were grasslands. Leopard geckos are quite adaptable, and although their primary habitat is desert, they can adapt to slightly different ones.

Predators also are adaptable, and a variety of predators prey on wild leopard geckos, from foxes and jackals to wild cats of various types to birds and other reptiles. Therefore, leopard geckos have a couple of behaviors they use often to protect themselves from becoming breakfast, lunch or dinner for a hungry predator.

First and foremost, leopard geckos hide. Rocks, vegetation and variations in the terrain can all provide hiding spots, as do deserted rodent burrows. If no other hole is available, sometimes leopard geckos dig their own. By hiding in small places, the geckos can use their large eyes and excellent vision to watch for both potential meals for themselves and to avoid becoming a meal.

When they move from a hiding spot, geckos will terrain to shield themselves from visibility. A dip in the soil, a pile of rocks, or a line of dry grasses can all provide cover. The leopard gecko's coloring aids in their ability to hide; the light coloring with dark spots helps them blend into natural terrain, gravel, and dry grasses.

Hiding spots are vital to a leopard gecko's well-being, both in captivity and in the wild. Without hiding spots, a leopard gecko feels vulnerable and stressed.

Living as a nocturnal animal

Survival in a desert environment can be chancy at best. Not only does the gecko living in the desert need to protect herself from the sun, heat, and dehydration, but she must find food to eat and enough water to survive. Many desert animals have coped by sleeping during the day and becoming active at night when the environment cools as the sun goes down. Although many people think cold-blooded creatures such as reptiles are more active during the day when the sun is out, the sun can actually become too warm, and in climates where that can happen, being nocturnal is much safer for survival.

In the desert, leopard geckos, as insectivores, find food better at night because many of the desert insects are also nocturnal. Insects, too, can dehydrate (or even cook!) in the extremely hot temperatures during the day.

Being nocturnal also saves energy. Too much movement burns up calories and when food is scarce, saving that energy is important. By sleeping during the day, and not moving until it's time to hunt or prey is sighted, less energy is expended. This vital survival trait can also be seen in captivity. Although you may think a sleeping leopard gecko is lazy, she really isn't. This trait saved many of her ancestors from starving when food was hard to find.

When living with us, leopard geckos are often disturbed during the day, and their sleep cycle is disrupted. Disrupting their sleep cycle can ultimately lead to stress and resulting health problems. Leopard geckos should be allowed to sleep undisturbed during the day as much as possible. However, during the evening hours, as the sun sets and the geckos would naturally begin to be more active, you can interact with them.

Interpreting Communications

Leopard geckos do not speak as we do, obviously, but that doesn't mean they don't have some means of communication. They can speak their minds amazingly well.

Warning behaviors

Male leopard geckos fight, and sometimes the provocation can be very slight although most fights are over territory and breeding rights. If a male leopard gecko is in his own territory and a strange male approaches, the defending male will bob his head up and down. This is his first communication, "Hey, guy, you're in my territory." If the trespassing male leaves, all is well again. The warning was issued and answered correctly. However, if the warning is ignored, the defending male will approach the intruder, walking tall, as he continues to bob his head.

During this threat display, the defending male may vocalize, making a series of clicks or squeaks. The intruder may or may not respond, depending upon how confident he is. The defending male will then open his mouth wide, showing the intruder how big his mouth is and how much damage he will inflict upon him. Many fights will stop at this point, with no damage to either male.

However, if the intruder doesn't back off, a fight will ensue and both can be severely injured.

You can see some of this warning behavior with your pet leopard gecko. If you startle her and pick her up by grabbing, she may open her mouth wide as if to bite you. She really doesn't have any desire to bite you; she's simply warning you, "Hey! Don't do that!"

 A leopard gecko who feels she's in danger of being eaten, such as being threatened by the family dog, will scream amazingly loud. She can sound like a baby screaming, and that scream can be distracting enough to allow the gecko to escape.

Courting signals

When a male and female are introduced to each other during breeding season (usually the spring), the male will begin clicking to her, bobbing his head and circling her. His tail may twitch and bounce. He shows his excitement and willingness to breed by expending a lot of energy.

The female will often simply watch his antics, turning her head but otherwise not responding. Or she may stand up and turn as he circles her. Some leopard gecko breeders have said that occasionally a female will approach a male and begin bobbing her head, thereby initiating the breeding. The male is usually the instigator, however.

Enjoying life

Captive-bred leopard geckos are experts at enjoying life. They have food provided on a regular basis, have a wonderful home with all the amenities, and don't have to worry about predators. Life is good. They show their gratitude for all our efforts to make their world comfortable by sleeping! If a leopard gecko can figure out how to hang one or use it, there would be a hammock in every leopard gecko cage!

Actually, your leopard gecko's relaxation is the ultimate compliment. An animal in captivity who is stressed will not sleep as comfortably as most leopard geckos do. A stressed animal will pace, will try to escape, will not eat or will eat very little, and will not thrive. Although your new leopard gecko may try to escape from the cage initially, once the new environment is known, those attempts will stop.

If your new leopard gecko continues to try and escape after several days in the new cage, something is wrong. Make sure the gecko is not too visible or that something isn't threatening her — like the household cat.

Hunting habits

Captive leopard geckos do take great pleasure in their hunting escapades, and you can see that pleasure in their body language. A leopard gecko hunting a cricket watches the insect intently, tracks it with both eyes, and stands tall. As the cricket moves, the gecko's tail lifts and twitches. That tail twitch betrays his excitement. When the cricket is caught, the gecko is again relaxed.

Handling Your Gecko

People like to handle their pets; that's why we have pets. But although your leopard gecko may learn to tolerate handling, she will never learn to like it. We will always be a potential threat as far as your gecko is concerned, so our handling should be kept to a minimum. Taking the gecko out of her cage and holding her once a day is great; twice a day is okay; but three times a day is too many times for most geckos. Geckos are best enjoyed by appreciating them for what they are and by watching their behaviors in their cage.

Holding the gecko

An adult leopard gecko who is very secure with your handling can learn to ride on your shoulder as you move around the house, or sit on your shoulder as you read or work at the computer. As I'm typing these words into my computer, Grandpa, my oldest leopard gecko, is asleep on the top of my computer monitor. However, getting your gecko to this point takes lots of calm, gentle handling of short duration. You need to teach your gecko that she can trust you by keeping the following in mind when handling your gecko:

✔ Pick up your gecko by reaching around her body with your fingers and then cupping them around her. If she's young, untamed, and very fast, you can catch her by cupping both hands around her. Then cup her in your hands (see Figure 6-1). As you do this, let her see. If you hide her head in your hands, she will struggle even more.

WARNING!

✔ Never catch your gecko by her tail or pick her up by the tail. She can drop her tail in self-defense, and although this is natural, it's a big shock to her system.

✔ Be aware of her legs as you hold her. They are strong for her size, but if you bend one backwards in your hands, or squish one, you can potentially break it.

✔ Let your gecko grip your hand and fingers with her feet. Her nails are sharp and may prick your skin, but doing so makes her more secure.

Figure 6-1: Hold your gecko firmly but carefully, cupped in your hand.

Teaching children

Children have a tendency to grab hard at something that is wiggling. If the wiggler is a leopard gecko, that can be disastrous. So kids in the family need to be taught to hold a leopard gecko gently without squeezing when the gecko wiggles.

I taught my nephew how hard he could hold a gecko by having him hold my fingers. I held all four fingers of one hand close together and had him hold them. I then wiggled my fingers and told him, "Don't let them get away!" and as he tried to keep my fingers from getting away, I told him when he was holding too tight. After several practice sessions, he understood and is now able to get a gecko out of the cage and hold it by himself.

Making Baby Geckos

The decision to breed your geckos, or to allow your geckos to breed, is not one to be undertaken lightly. Consider the following:

- ✔ **Breeding can potentially shorten the life span of your female.** Females who were never bred have been known to live into their twenties, but those who reproduced are lucky to make it to 20 years old.

- ✔ **Breeding is not a money-making venture.** Don't breed leopard geckos with the idea of making money or paying for your hobby. You have to keep several dozen breeding geckos for that to happen.

- ✔ **Breeding takes some work on your part.** The eggs need to be incubated, and the babies need to be caged away from their parents.

- ✔ **You have to make sure you can find homes for all of the babies.** Although many people keep the first couple of baby geckos hatched, considering that a breeding pair can produce 8 to 10, maybe even 12 babies per year, you have to have a plan for the rest of the babies. Although selling the babies can sometimes be an option, you won't find a big market for one or two babies. Most suppliers and stores want to buy several at a time. And baby geckos don't sell for very much because they're too tiny and fragile.

Check with your local reptile store. Although they probably get most of their leopard geckos directly from breeders, they may be able to take your babies for store credit. You can use that toward cricket or mealworm purchases.

If, you still think you'd enjoy breeding geckos, the following sections explain the best way to breed.

Choosing the best breeding stock

Of course, if you plan on breeding, you want to breed the best stock you can find; so, keep these basics in mind so you choose the best of the breed:

✔ **Get one male and at least one female.** If there is only one female, the male may pester her constantly. With two or three females, his attentions can be shared.

Although getting one of each sex sounds obvious, figuring out which gecko is which sex can be very difficult to determine with babies; so, you're better off starting with young adults. Male leopard geckos are usually heavier bodied than females, with a bigger, wider head, but this isn't always apparent in young adults. So to determine the sex, you need to flip them over and look at the private parts.

Males have a chevron shaped series of pores in the skin between the back legs and females do not. Males also have two swellings at the base of the tail just past the vent (also called the cloaca). Females do not have these two swellings.

✔ **Your breeding geckos should be strong, fat (but not obese), and healthy.** Use the guidelines offered in Chapter 3 to select the healthiest geckos you can find.

✔ **Breeding geckos should be at least 18 to 24 months of age before you begin using them for breeding.** They are not fully mature until this age.

✔ **Decide whether you want to breed for colors or patterns.** Take that into consideration as you choose your breeding stock.

✔ **Feed your breeding stock well after bringing them home.** Make sure they are chubby with fat tails and have adjusted well to their new cages.

✔ **Keep the males and females separate.**

Cooling comes before heat

In the wild, breeding follows the shortened days and cooler temperatures of winter. In captivity, this can be duplicated by turning off the lights to your geckos in the late fall, shortening their daylight hours. You can also cool their cage slightly by taking the incandescent light or ceramic heater off the cage. Keep the undertank heater, though, as you don't want to cool them too much. After about four to six weeks, begin turning the lights off later and later, again, duplicating the lengthening daylight hours of spring. At this point, you can increase the heat in the cage, too, by putting the ceramic heater back on top.

Leopard geckos have been bred in captivity for so many generations that some breeders have been able to bypass this period of reduced daylight and cooler temperatures. You can try it either way.

Doing what comes naturally

Once the cooling period is over (if you decide to do that) or if you don't cool them, when spring arrives, introduce the male to the females. A good way to do it without too much stress is to clean the females' cage. With new bedding, rearranged hiding spots and new furnishings, it becomes a whole new cage and is no longer the girls' territory. When you put them back in the clean cage, put the male in, too.

Breeding may or may not happen right away. Some males will see the girls and immediately begin courting. These males will circle the female, twitch their tail, and bob the head. Other males will wait until dark.

 When the mating act occurs, the male will grab the female by the skin on the back of her neck to hold her. Watch your females for bite wounds on the back of the neck. If you find any, dab on some antibiotic ointment daily until the wounds heal.

Laying eggs

As the eggs develop in the female's abdomen, they show through her thin white belly skin. When she's ready to lay, she will be bulging obviously, and you'll need to give her a place to lay her eggs. I like to use small covered plastic containers; something larger than a margarine container but smaller than a shoebox works well. Cut a hole in the side so that she can easily get in. Smooth the plastic edges so she doesn't hurt herself.

Put 1½ to 2 inches (3.8 to 5 centimeters) of dampened vermiculite in the box. Laying females often betray themselves by digging up the vermiculite and spreading it all over. Two eggs are laid each time (each set is referred to as a *clutch*), both in the same hole. The newly laid eggs are soft and somewhat sticky. Fertile eggs quickly become stiff and while not as hard as chicken eggs, they will be much stiffer than when first laid. When you pick up the newly laid eggs, do not rotate them. Unlike bird eggs, reptile eggs must remain right side up or the developing embryo can be harmed or even killed.

During breeding season, it's best to check the vermiculite daily for eggs. Use a spoon to gently lift the vermiculite. Do not rotate the eggs once you find them.

A young female will lay two to three clutches of two eggs each her first breeding year while larger older females may have five to six clutches of two eggs each.

Incubating eggs

You can incubate eggs using one of the following methods:

- ✔ The eggs can be incubated in a plastic margarine container with an inch (2.5 centimeters) of moist vermiculite in the bottom. The vermiculite should be damp with most of the water drained out. Punch five or six holes in the lid of the container for some air flow.

- ✔ Some people have been able to incubate leopard geckos without using an incubator; they place the container with the eggs in a warm but not hot location such as above the refrigerator.

- ✔ An incubator provides a more reliable, steady source of heat for incubating eggs. You can buy one; just ask at your local reptile specialty store, check out the reptile supply catalogs online, or look for advertisements in any reptile magazines.

Incubation temperatures have an effect on the sex of the offspring. At 79 degrees Fahrenheit (26 degrees Celsius), most of the offspring will be female. At 86 degrees Fahrenheit (30 degrees Celsius), there will be a mix of male and female. At 90 degrees Fahrenheit (32 degrees Celsius), most of the offspring will be male.

Be sure to place the eggs in the incubator in the same position that you found them (right side up).

Watching babies hatch

Babies will poke their noses through their egg shells in 50 to 60 days. A baby first cuts a slit in the egg with the tip of the nose and then rests for a little while. Don't try to help; the baby will leave when she's ready. When the baby finally decides to leave the egg, sometimes as long as a day after slitting the eggshell, she'll leave in a hurry.

When you pick up the baby from the incubation container, be care-ful. These little guys are fast and tiny. Little leopard geckos are also feisty; they will open their mouths, try to bite you, hiss, and squeak at you (see Figure 6-2).

Babies should be put in their own cage away from the parents. If the cage has lots of hiding places, several babies can be housed together.

Figure 6-2: Baby geckos are very cute, very active, and amazingly brave.

Raising babies

Most commercial leopard gecko breeders house babies in individ-ual shoebox-type containers using paper towels as substrate. This allows for ease of care, each baby can be identified (as to parentage, date of birth, and so forth), and make for easy cleaning.

Most pet owners prefer to do more for their pets, especially their first hatchlings. So if you want to set up a nice cage, go ahead. The babies can live in the same conditions as their parents. Just make sure there are plenty of hiding spots.

The babies won't eat for a few days; they're living off the remnants of their yolk sacs. They'll shed for the first time a few days after hatching, and after they shed they'll be hungry. Offer baby crickets (two to three weeks old) and baby mealworms. Your reptile store can get these for you. Dust the crickets with vitamin/mineral powder twice a week and calcium once a week.

Keep a shallow saucer or jar lid with water in the cage, and mist the side of each hiding place once a day to increase the humidity a little.

Chapter 7

Keeping Your Gecko Healthy

· ·

· ·

*Y*our leopard gecko has the potential to live a long life (20 years or more) but as a pet, he has no control over what happens. You have the ability and responsibility to keep your pet happy, active, well-fed and healthy. But don't worry, although that sounds like a lot of responsibility, I give you enough information in this chapter to make it easy for you.

Envisioning a Healthy Leopard Gecko

Sometimes, your gecko may be injured, come down with an illness, or catch a parasite. You won't be able to tell if something's wrong with your gecko if you don't have a picture in your mind of a healthy one. So before we go on to discuss health problems, let's take a look at a healthy leopard gecko.

Weighing your gecko in your hand

A healthy gecko feels like he weighs more than he actually does. It feels like the little gecko's skin is full of something heavier than water — like tiny little fishing weights, maybe. In your hand, the gecko will also feel strong, and even if he's calm in your hand, he should feel like he's able to struggle against you. This weight and vigor are important; they show that your gecko is healthy.

 If you have a scale for small items that weighs in grams, you can actually weigh your gecko on a regular basis (once a week is fine) and keep track of his weight.

Feeling the skin and contours

The skin on the top of the body is covered with little granular scales so the skin is bumpy. The skin on the underside of the body is smooth. The tail is ringed and lumpy. When you gently run your hands over your gecko and feel his body, there should be no unexpected lumps or bumps under the skin; at least none that are not part of the skeletal structure underneath. The contours of the body are uniform and symmetrical.

Be very gentle and extremely careful when handling the tail. Remember, you lizard can drop his tail if he feels threatened.

Checking out the legs, feet, and toes

Your leopard gecko's legs look too small for his body, but they're stronger than they look and do the job he needs them to do. Although small, they should be well muscled with little muscle bulges on both the front and back legs. The bones of the legs are straight.

The wrists should be bent correctly so the gecko walks on the bottoms of his feet, and the toes of the feet should be well spread out. Each toe has a tiny little claw that helps him grip the ground he's walking or running on, and the bristles on the bottom of his feet help, too.

Examining the face

Leopard geckos often look as though they are smiling. Although I know that is because of the way their face is constructed and the size of their mouth, I still like to think they're happy! Especially my leopard geckos!

The most prominent features on a leopard gecko's face are his eyes. The eyes are very large, almost oversized, for his face. They are clear and clean and the eyelids well fitted to the eyes. The nostrils are also clear and clean, and when the gecko breathes, his breaths are easy and clear. The jaws are large, too, and fit together well, making the mouth close with a smooth line. The earholes can be open (if the gecko is relaxed and warm) or closed (if he's cool or stressed).

Knowing normal behavior

It's important to watch your gecko enough so that you know what his normal behaviors are. Watch him in the evening when he's more active and when he hunts crickets. See how he stalks the waxworms in the shallow saucer in his cage, grabs and crushes them and then manages to swallow them even though they can be large.

Make sure you also know where in the cage your gecko normally sleeps during the day. He may have a sleeping place at the warm end of his cage and another in a cooler spot. Learn his normal habits.

Preventing (and Solving) Problems

Pet ownership does not always run smoothly, especially when keeping reptiles as pets. We are keeping an animal in a situation that is not totally natural, feeding him foods he may not have eaten in the wild, and handling him. Keeping reptiles captive as pets does sometimes cause problems. Of course, it prevents problems, too. Well cared for captives live much longer than their wild counterparts who face drought, seasonal floods, hunger and predators. So there is a balance here. We can't do anything to help the wild geckos but we can make life easier for our pets.

Watching for what's different

The best way to catch a problem early is to watch for what's different. When you know what your gecko's body feels like you can spot when something has changed. If you pick him up one day and feel a bump under the skin on one of his sides, you will know right away that bump is different because you know what his little body is like normally.

Watching for what's different in behavior can also give you clues as to your gecko's health. If, during his daytime sleeping, he normally moves back and forth between two spots in his cage (regulating his body temperature) but then begins to sleep only in the hot sections, you will know that's a change from his normal routine.

Changes happen for a reason — good or bad — so knowing what is normal can help you pinpoint those changes.

Getting rid of parasites

Luckily leopard geckos are not prone to many parasites, either internally or externally. They have been bred in captivity for so many years in clean conditions that many parasites are just simply not present any more. However, every once in a while a problem may occur.

Mites

Mites are tiny brown, black, or red bugs that look like moving specks. You may see them on the furnishings in your gecko's cage, on the substrate if you use paper towels, or actually on your lizard. Mites can be introduced by a new reptile; especially if the new reptile was in overcrowded or dirty conditions.

All new reptiles — leopard geckos or others — should be quarantined for at least a month prior to being introduced to your existing pets. This can cut down on transmission of parasites and diseases.

A bad mite infestation can lead to blood loss (due to repeated biting by the mites), anemia, and eventually death. The mites may look tiny, but they reproduce rapidly and can overwhelm a reptile.

You can get rid of mites by gently washing your reptile with soapy water. Take a very gentle soap and put it in your hands, making suds. Then pick up your gecko and gently soap him. Rinse him well, getting all the soap off of him.

Then thoroughly clean the old cage, using a diluted bleach solution on all of the cage furnishings and the cage itself. Make sure all the corners, cracks and crevasses of the cage and its furnishings are scrubbed. Once everything is scrubbed, rinse everything well until the bleach smell is gone. Put in fresh substrate and then set the cage up again. You may have to do this two or three times over the next few weeks before the mites are gone for good.

Coccidia

Coccidia are small protozoan parasites that live in the leopard gecko's intestinal tract. The first symptom is usually diarrhea, often with blood in it. Coccidia can be transmitted from one gecko to another rapidly in a captive situation as each gecko in the same cage is exposed to the feces of each other. This parasite is passed through the feces.

Coccidia leads to dehydration, anemia, secondary infections and if untreated, death. Veterinary care is needed to determine whether coccidian is indeed the culprit, and to prescribe appropriate medication.

A veterinarian specializing in reptile medicine in your area can be found at the Web site for the Association of Reptilian and Amphibian Veterinarians www.arav.org.

You also need to separate all of the affected leopard geckos, putting each in his own cage, at least during treatment. Use paper towels as substrate and keep the cages very clean. Pick up all eliminations as soon as you can. Do not put them back together until all have received a clean bill of health.

Crypto

Crypto is the commonly used shorthand for *cryptosporidium,* an internal parasite. This is a particularly deadly parasite; there is no cure, and leopard geckos infected by it will die. The geckos stop eating, they lose all of their fat reserves and eventually die.

Crypto shows up first in the stools so any unusual-looking stools should be taken to the vet for analysis. The second symptom is a loss of muscle tone in the legs. If you have a gecko who shows odd stools and a loss of muscle tone, immediately quarantine him from your other geckos. It may already be too late — it may have been transmitted already — but separate them anyway, just in case it hasn't yet spread.

Many people who have bought leopard geckos at reptile expos or shows have learned later that they have introduced crypto to their home gecko populations. To protect yourself and your geckos, never buy a thin or unthrifty looking gecko. Always quarantine new geckos for a minimum of one month although a longer quarantine is safer and if you have any questions or doubt, take a stool sample in to your veterinarian.

Avoiding other problems

Leopard geckos are, on the whole, healthy little lizards. Most of the problems seen in leopard geckos are due to poor husbandry. Temperatures may be incorrect, foods may be lacking in nutrition, or the cage may be constantly dirty. In short, many of these problems are preventable with good care.

Hypocalcemia

Hypocalcemia is also known as metabolic bone disease. A gecko suffering from hypocalcemia may have a swollen jaw, swollen legs, may walk on the backs of his feet, and will be lethargic. When he walks, he may appear to be "swimming" — throwing his legs and feet forward rather than walking correctly.

Hypocalcemia is due to a lack of calcium and vitamin D3. If the gecko receives the supplements recommended in Chapter 5 on a regular schedule (once to twice a week) and the insects he eats are gut-loaded, this disease can be prevented.

Skin wounds

Breaks in the skin can occur during breeding season (when the male grabs the female by the skin on the back of his neck), during scuffles between cagemates, or may just be accidents moving around the cage. Normally, small scrapes are not a problem; a touch of an antibiotic ointment is normally all that's needed. However, watch for infections. If the skin appears to be swollen and inflamed, remove that gecko and house him separately for a while. Use paper towels as a substrate so you can keep him very clean. Wash and treat the wound daily until it heals.

Polysporin and Neosporin topical antibiotic ointments can be safely used on leopard gecko wounds.

Stomatitis

Stomatitis, often called mouth rot, is an infection in the mouth. The jaw is usually swollen, the jaws may be uneven, and the gecko will refuse to eat. If you can open the jaws, pus can be seen in the mouth.

Stomatitis can have several causes. Lower than optimal cage temperatures can lead to a suppressed immune system, leaving the gecko open to disease. Injuries to the mouth can also let the bacteria of stomatitis take hold. In leopard geckos, fighting with cagemates is the most common cause of mouth rot.

The gecko suffering from mouth rot must be separated from his cagemates and housed individually. The mouth can be cleaned with diluted Betadine, but a veterinarian needs to be consulted for systemic antibiotics. While your gecko is being treated, increase the temperature in his cage about 5 degrees; this will help his immune system cope. You can do this by putting a towel over or around about half of the cage. The towel will reduce heat loss.

Respiratory infections

When temperatures in a reptile's cage are kept too cool for a period of time, the reptile's immune system will become weakened and vulnerable. Leopard gecko's are prone to respiratory infections when conditions are too cool. The first signs may include the sounds of wheezing and labored breathing, and you will see a discharge from the nose.

In milder cases, just raising the cage temperatures to the correct temperatures may be enough (85 to 90 degrees Fahrenheit/29 to 32 degrees Celsius at the hot end of the cage). If that doesn't clear it up in a few days, consult your veterinarian.

Getting Vet Care for Your Gecko

A veterinarian is your partner in your gecko's health care. Although some people seem to feel that a pet this small and this inexpensive doesn't need vet care; that attitude is wrong. Leopard geckos didn't ask to be kept in captivity, and as their keepers, it's our job to help them live out their life span in health and comfort. Often a veterinarian is needed to help them do that.

Finding a vet

Not all veterinarians specialize or are even knowledgeable in reptile medicine. Reptiles are very different from mammals, even mammals of the same size, and their care is different. Drugs often work very differently in a cold-blooded creature's system and even those that do work, are needed in different dosages. You need to find a vet in your area who knows all about reptiles and when stumped with a problem, knows where to find help himself.

To find a veterinarian who specializes in reptiles, you can contact the Association of Reptilian and Amphibian Veterinarians at www.arav.org. This non-profit organization's goal is to improve veterinary care and husbandry for all reptiles and amphibians kept in captivity. It is best to find a reptile vet before an emergency occurs. This gives you some time to shop around to find a veterinarian with whom you feel comfortable. It also gives the vet a chance to get to know your gecko and his medical history. If you wait until an emergency happens, you will be scrambling to find a reptile vet who can see you right away.

Deciding when to call the vet

If in doubt, call! If, at any time, you feel there is a problem with your leopard gecko that you don't understand, call your veterinarian.

Call your vet if:

- Your gecko appears to have a broken limb.
- Your gecko has a problem with an eye (swollen, enlarged, closed, or oozing)

- Your gecko has a discharge from the nose or dried matter around the nose.

- Your gecko has a swollen jaw, uneven or open mouth, or has pus in the mouth.

- Your gecko has soft, different or bloody feces.

- Your gecko has diarrhea, a swollen cloaca or anything protruding from the cloaca.

- Your gecko is bleeding, and it doesn't stop quickly.

Your veterinarian will charge you for his services; that is, after all, his job. But you may also be saving your gecko's life. So call.

Performing basic first aid

Luckily, leopard geckos don't have many first-aid needs. When kept in a good environment properly furnished, there aren't many ways that a gecko can hurt himself. Most injuries come from cagemates and since most leopard geckos get along (at least the girls do, anyway) even those injuries are rare.

In all cases, immediately separate the gecko from his cagemates and house individually until healed. Use paper towel as a substrate as it is clean and easily discarded.

Here are a few suggestions for some problems that may happen:

- **Bleeding:** Minor bleeding will stop on its own rather quickly. After all, a tiny gecko cannot afford to lose much blood! However, if the bleeding doesn't stop right away, use a cotton-tipped stick to put some pressure on the wound. (Careful! Not too much pressure.) If the bleeding continues, get the gecko to your vet.

- **Bite wounds:** Clean bite wounds with some soap and water or diluted Betadine and then dab on a touch of antibiotic ointment. Treat daily until it heals.

- **Broken limbs:** Legs usually don't break unless there's some major trauma or the gecko is suffering from metabolic bone disease. In either case, keep the gecko quiet and call your vet.

- **Detached tail:** Keep the gecko quiet, offer food and water, dab on some antibiotic ointment, and let the wound heal.

An injury or illness is not necessarily a death sentence for your leopard gecko. There is a lot that can be done to help him. So do what you can, then don't be afraid to call for help.

Shedding Is Natural

Leopard geckos shed their skin, as do all lizards and all other reptiles. The frequency that this happens depends upon how quickly your gecko is growing and your gecko's overall health. Newly hatched geckos will shed the first time just a few days after hatching. Rapidly growing young geckos may shed every other week during growth spurts, or it may be several weeks in between. The schedule for shedding is very individual to each lizard.

Many cultures recognized the uniqueness of shedding the entire skin and created legends, myths and beliefs around it. Some cultures consider it a rebirth, as the new skin underneath is fresh and new — looking like a new creature. Other cultures felt that the ability to shed the old body covering was a symbol of longevity — a creature that constantly produced a new skin never died. Legends and myths aside, there is nothing mystical about this process.

Shedding happens

As the skin on the gecko's body gets ready to shed, it becomes milky and opaque. The gecko will look silvery and dull in color. When the new layer of skin underneath is fully formed, the old skin will begin to detach from the new skin below it. It will get loose, and pieces will peel off. (A good comparison is the peeling that people do after a bad sunburn.)

As the old skin peels, the gecko will reach around, grab the skin, pull it off and eat it. No one really knows why this skin is eaten, but many suspect it may be the gecko's way of saving whatever nutrients may remain in the old skin (see Figure 7-1). Others feel that by eating the skin instead of leaving it on the ground as snakes do, the gecko is removing signs of his presence, thereby trying to avoid discovery by predators.

Once the old skin is off, the gecko will be bright and shiny. The new skin is at its most colorful immediately after shedding.

Figure 7-1: Although myths abound concerning reptiles' shedding, it is natural.

Preventing shedding problems

If a gecko does not shed completely, leaving small pieces attached, the new skin underneath will be harmed. When that skin then needs to shed, layers of unshed skin will build. Eventually serious harm will result.

If a gecko is too dry, the skin may not shed well; it may stick to the skin underneath. In Chapter 5, we discussed the need for humidity in your gecko's hiding spots; this is one reason why that's so important. By misting his hiding spot once a day, you increased the humidity. That dampness helps the old skin to detach and come off. Now, just because the humidity in his hiding hole is good doesn't mean the whole cage should be humid! No, the gecko is a desert creature but those holes he hides in get humid when the water condenses. By misting his cage hiding spot, we are trying to recreate those conditions.

A gecko who is not eating well may also have problems shedding. Those vitamin/mineral supplements are important to maintaining and growing healthy skin. In addition, when the crickets and mealworms are fed well before the gecko eats them, he then gets the nutrition they were provided.

If your gecko has shed by himself but has a few pieces of skin stuck to him, you can help him. Take a covered plastic container and put a handful of paper towels in the bottom. Dampen the paper towels with warm (not hot) water. They can be pretty wet. Put the gecko in the container for about 15 minutes and then check those pieces of skin. They should slide right off.

If he has some pieces of skin that do not come off with the dampness, do not pull them off; that can tear the skin underneath. Instead, dab some antibiotic ointment on them and let it sit for a few minutes, then try to slide the skin off. You can rotate the ointment and the damp container treatment until the skin comes off.

During shedding, make sure all the old skin is off the toes. If it's not shed, the old skin can cut off circulation to the toes, causing toe loss.

Keeping Your Gecko's Tail Intact

Many lizards can drop their tail (called *autotomy*) in emergencies. They will do so if a predator threatens to grab them because the dropped tail will continue to twitch, hopefully distracting the predator. If grabbed by the tail, the tail will remain with the predator, and the lizard can then escape.

Dropping the tail

The tail disconnects from the body via *caudal (tail) fracture points* These are spots in the tail where the vertebrae will disconnect, tissues will split, and when the tail separates, the blood vessels will close off. Often there is very little blood loss.

Leopard geckos can do this, too, but losing a tail is not as simple as just dropping it — like a cut fingernail. The tail is a fat reserve for the lizard, and the loss of the tail can be a shock to the gecko's system. Although losing the tail will not kill the gecko, it can slow down growth or breeding efforts significantly.

Never ever grab a leopard gecko by the tail. Even a calm adult may drop its tail when grabbed suddenly or lifted by the tail.

Growing a new tail

If your leopard gecko drops his tail, he may regrow a new one. He needs to be housed individually, fed well and kept quiet. This is a severe shock to his system, and he needs to recuperate; it's just like any other major injury.

The new tail won't be nearly as nice as the original, however. For one thing, there won't be any vertebrae in it; the bones don't regrow. Instead the stiffness will be made from a growth of cartilage.

The shape of the new tail is often very different, too. Instead of being long and tube-like with a bulge in the middle, the new tail may be more round, like a small beach ball. Sometimes, a regrown tail looks like a second head (see Figure 7-2).

If threatened again, this second tail can be dropped, too, but new tails will not just keep growing indefinitely. Each subsequent tail will be smaller and more deformed. In addition, if tails are continuously lost, each incident will be a shock to the lizard. Eventually, the lizard's health will suffer.

Figure 7-2: A regrown tail rarely looks as good as the original and is usually deformed.

Ten Great Gecko Internet Sites

*T*he popularity of leopard geckos has resulted in many great Web sites for the species, as well as a wealth of information.

✔ **Photos and Care Sheet**
Ron Tremper is the co-author of "The Leopard Gecko Manual" (AVS, 2001) and is known for his brightly colored leopard geckos. www.leopardgecko.com

✔ **Leopard Gecko Information**
Melissa Kaplan offers some good information on leopard geckos and their care. www.anapsid.org/leaopardgek.html

✔ **More Photos**
Ray Hine is a leopard gecko breeder and has produced some beautiful geckos. www.rayhine.com

✔ **Sexing Geckos**
This site has an excellent description and photos about sexing males and females. www.reptilecare./leopardgender.html

✔ **The Berkley Geckos**
Spot lives in Berkley; here's his story.
www.lhs.Berkley.edu/biolab/wlhleopardgecko.html

✔ **Photo Gallery**
You can never see too many beautiful leopard gecko photos.
www.repticzone.com/photogallery/leopardgeckos7.html

✔ **Everything Geckos**
Everything and more about care, breeding, and health.
www.drgecko.com

✔ **British Gecko Forum**
This is an interesting and often informative e-mail forum.
www.geckoworld.co.uk/forum

✔ **Interesting Colors and Patterns**
Here are some photos of leopard gecko colors and color patterns. www.mountaingecko.freeservers.com/photo4.html

✔ **Gecko Health**
An informative look at leopard gecko health.
www.thegeckospot.com/leohealth.html

Ten Sources for Everything Reptile

Sometimes it can be tough to find stuff for reptiles; luckily, the Internet has made the world smaller. Here are some great sources for cages, crickets, mealworms, books, and much more.

✔ **Reptile Supplies**
LLL Reptile carries just about everything a reptile owner needs, and if it doesn't carry it — just ask! www.lllreptile.com

✔ **More Reptile Supplies**
Big Apple Herp has substrates, cage furnishings, and more. www.bigappleherp.com

✔ **Information Galore**
Melissa Kaplan is the reptile expert for the Veterinary Information Network. www.anapsid.org

✔ **Reptile Veterinarians**
Here's how to find a veterinarian who specializes in reptiles. www.arav.org

✔ **Crickets and Mealworms**
A supplier for crickets and mealworms in small orders or bulk. www.rainbowmealworms.com

✔ **Reptiles Magazine**
A resource for everything reptiles. www.animalnetwork.com/reptiles/home.aspx

✔ **Books About Reptiles**
Find old and new books about reptiles. www.herpbooks.com

✔ **More Reptile Books**
A variety of reptile books including some very in-depth studies. www.web4u.com/kreiger-publishing/

✔ **Custom Reptile Cages**
Some beautiful and functional custom-built cages. www.cagesbydesign.com

✔ **Vision Cages**
Stackable, one-piece cages with sliding front door. www.lllreptile.com

Index

FOR DUMMIES

Pet care essentials in plain English

DOG BREEDS

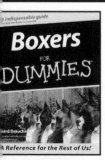

The indispensable guide

Boxers
FOR DUMMIES

A Reference for the Rest of Us!

0-7645-5285-6

The indispensable guide

German Shepherds
FOR DUMMIES

D. Caroline Coile, Ph.D.

A Reference for the Rest of Us!

0-7645-5280-5

"A gold mine of information...."

Golden Retrievers
FOR DUMMIES

A Reference for the Rest of Us!

0-7645-5267-8

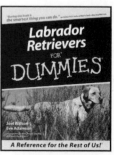

"Buying this book is the smartest thing you can do."

Labrador Retrievers
FOR DUMMIES

Joel Walton
Eve Adamson

A Reference for the Rest of Us!

0-7645-5281-3

fun and easy way to
ext, train, and care for your Pug

Pugs
FOR DUMMIES

Reference for the Rest of Us!

0-7645-54076-9

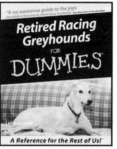

"A no-nonsense guide to the joys
and pitfalls of adopting the retired racing Greyhound."

Retired Racing Greyhounds
FOR DUMMIES

A Reference for the Rest of Us!

0-7645-5276-7

Siberian Huskies
FOR DUMMIES

Diane Morgan

A Reference for the Rest of Us!

0-7645-5279-1

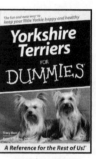

The fun and easy way to
keep your little Yorkie happy and healthy

Yorkshire Terriers
FOR DUMMIES

Tracy Barr

A Reference for the Rest of Us!

0-7645-6880-9

Also available:

Jack Russell Terriers For Dummies
(0-7645-5268-6)

Rottweilers For Dummies
(0-7645-5271-6)

Chihuahuas For Dummies
(0-7645-5284-8)

Dachshunds For Dummies
(0-7645-5289-9)

Pit Bulls For Dummies
(0-7645-5291-0)

DOG CARE, HEALTH, TRAINING, & BEHAVIOR

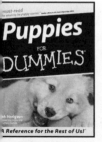

must-read

Puppies
FOR DUMMIES

A Reference for the Rest of Us!

0-7645-5255-4

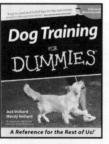

"Easy to read and full of tips for the new owner,
as well as the experienced one."

Dog Training
FOR DUMMIES

Jack Volhard
Wendy Volhard

A Reference for the Rest of Us!

0-7645-5286-4

"This book is just what the geriatric vet ordered."

Senior Dogs
FOR DUMMIES

A Reference for the Rest of Us!

0-7645-5818-8

Also available:

Choosing a Dog For Dummies
(0-7645-5310-0)

Dog Health & Nutrition For Dummies
(0-7645-5318-6)

Dog Tricks For Dummies
(0-7645-5287-2)

House Training For Dummies
(0-7645-5349-6)

Dogs For Dummies, 2nd Edition
(0-7645-5274-0)

FOR DUMMIES®

Pet care essentials in plain English

CATS & KITTENS

0-7645-5275-9 0-7645-4150-1

BIRDS

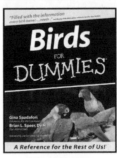

0-7645-5139-6 0-7645-5311-9

AMPHIBIANS & REPTILES

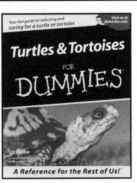

0-7645-2569-7 0-7645-5313-5 0-7645-5260-0

FISH & AQUARIUMS

0-7645-5156-6 0-7645-5340-2

SMALL ANIMALS

0-7645-5259-7 0-7645-0861-X